THE
DYNASTIES OF THE KANARESE DISTRICTS OF THE BOMBAY PRESIDENCY

THE
DYNASTIES OF THE KANARESE DISTRICTS OF THE BOMBAY PRESIDENCY

FROM THE

EARLIEST HISTORICAL TIMES TO THE MUHAMMADAN CONQUEST OF A.D. 1318

BY

J. F. FLEET,

Of H. M.'s Bombay Convenanted Civil Service, Member of the Royal Asiatic Society of Great Britain and Ireland, and of the Bombay Branch of the Royal Asiatic Society, and Fellow of the University of Bombay.

(Written for the Bombay Gazetteer)

GYAN

Published by

GYAN

Gyan Publishing House
5, Ansari Road
Daryaganj, New Delhi-110002
Phone: 011-47034999, 9811692060
E-mail: books@gyanbooks.com

Distribution Network
gyanbooks.com
India, USA, Canada, UK, Australia, France

ISBN : 978-81-212-4515-9 (HB)
First Published, 1882

2nd Impression 2020

Printed at: Gyan Press, Delhi.

THE

DYNASTIES OF THE KANARESE DISTRICTS

OF THE

BOMBAY PRESIDENCY

FROM THE

EARLIEST HISTORICAL TIMES TO THE MUHAMMADAN CONQUEST OF A.D. 1318.

BY

J. F. FLEET,

Of H. M.'s Bombay Covenanted Civil Service, Member of the Royal Asiatic Society of Great Britain and Ireland, and of the Bombay Branch of the Royal Asiatic Society, and Fellow of the University of Bombay.

(Written for the Bombay Gazetteer.)

Bombay:

PRINTED AT THE GOVERNMENT CENTRAL PRESS.

1882.

SECTION I.

INTRODUCTORY.

No authentic work of a definite historical character has ever been written by the Hindus of Western India. But, in the inscriptions on copper-plates and stone-tablets, on monumental stones, the pedestals of idols, the walls and pillars of temples, and rocks, there have come down to us, particularly in the Kanarese country, a large number of original historical records of the most important kind. In these records, if they could be exhaustively examined, there exist abundant materials for compiling a detailed and connected history of the Kanarese districts of the Bombay Presidency, and of the neighbouring territories of Madras, Maisûr, and Haidarábád, from about the middle of the fifth to the end of the sixteenth century A.D., and, at the same time, for illustrating the development of the modern forms of the alphabets and of the vernacular language, the decay of old and the growth of new forms of religion, the origin of many of the different land-tenures and territorial divisions that now exist, and many other subjects of historical and antiquarian interest and importance.

The first systematic collection of these inscriptions was made by Sir Walter Elliot, K.C.S.I., who, when in the Madras Civil Service, was employed for a long time in this part of the country. Besides a large number of facsimile impressions of copper-plate grants, of which only a few have as yet been published, he compiled manuscript copies of no less than five hundred and ninety-five stone-tablet inscriptions from the Kanarese country alone and in the Sanskrit and Old-Kanarese languages, in addition to a large number of others from the Telugu country and in the Telugu language. The results of his labours were published in his paper on *Hindu Inscriptions*, which appeared first in the *Journal of the Royal Asiatic Society*, Old Series, Vol. IV., pp. 1 &c., and was afterwards reprinted, with corrections and additions, in the *Madras Journal of Literature and Science*, Vol. VII., pp. 193 &c.[1] And one copy of his collection of inscriptions from the Kanarese country, in two volumes entitled *Carnátakadesa Inscriptions* and belonging to the Library of the Edinburgh University, is at present in my hands.[2] The voluminous contents of these two books have as yet only very partially been made public.

---

1 The present paper is written upon much the same lines. No better method than Sir Walter Elliot's of dealing with the subject could well be devised.

2 These volumes will be quoted in this paper as the Elliot *MS. Collection*, Vol. I. and Vol. II. Three other copies of his collection appear to have been made; one of them is in the Library of the Royal Asiatic Society; but what became of the other two, I do not know. Many of the original copper-plate grants are now in his possession, and have been examined and transcribed for future publication by myself.

In 1865 the Maisur Government published a photographic collection of one hundred and fifty inscriptions on stone-tablets and copper-plates at Chitaldurg, Balagámve, Harihar, and other places in Maisur, from negatives taken by Major Dixon, H. M.'s 22nd Regiment, M. N. I. And in 1866, the Honourable Mr. Hope, Bo.C.S., edited for, and at the cost of, the Committee of Architectural Antiquities of Western India, under the title of *Inscriptions in Dharwar and Mysore*, a series of sixty-four photographic copies of inscriptions in the Belgaum, Dhárwád, Kaládgi, and North Kanara Districts of the Bombay Presidency, and in the neighbouring parts of the Madras Presidency and Maisur, from negatives taken by Dr. Pigou, Bo.M.S., and Col. Biggs, R.A.;[1] and a few other inscriptions, from negatives taken by the same gentlemen, were inserted by him in another work, entitled *Architecture in Dharwar and Mysore*, edited by him at the same time. These two collections being out of print and difficult to obtain, and the negatives being available at the India Office, the contents of them were re-arranged by myself and compiled, with additions, into one volume, which was published by the India Office in 1878, under the title of *Páli, Sanskrit, and Old-Canarese Inscriptions, from the Bombay Presidency and parts of the Madras Presidency and Maisur.*[2]

Meanwhile a few detached inscriptions had been published by Sir Walter Elliot, in the *Madras Journal of Literature and Science*,—by Mr. Wathen and Professor Dowson, in the early volumes of the *Journal of the Royal Asiatic Society*,—by Bál Gangádhar Sástri and General Sir George LeGrand Jacob, in the early volumes of the *Journal of the Bombay Branch of the Royal Asiatic Society*,—and by Dr. Taylor, in the *Transactions of the Literary Society of Bombay*.[3]

These publications, however, were desultory and few and far between; and it was not till the *Indian Antiquary* was started by Dr. Burgess, in 1872, that any real impetus was given to the study of the Epigraphy of Western India. Since then, in that Journal and in Dr. Burgess' *Archæological Reports*, as well as in the later volumes of the *Journal of the Bombay Branch of the Royal Asiatic Society*, a large number of most valuable inscriptions have been published, with texts and translations and in many instances with lithographic facsimiles, by Dr. Bühler, Professor Eggeling, the Revd. Mr. Kittel, Mr. Rice, the Revd. Mr. Foulkes, Prof. R. G. Bhándárkar, Pandit Bhagwánlál Indraji, and Messrs. S. P. Pandit and K. T. Telang, and, the large majority, by myself. And, in 1879, Mr. Rice published, under the title of *Mysore Inscriptions*, translations of all

---

1 Only ten copies of this work were published. Of these ten copies, one was presented to each of the following: the Royal Asiatic Society; the Société Asiatique at Paris; the German Oriental Society, Leipzig; the India Office Library; and Mr. Thomas, F.R.S.; and the remaining five were sent to Bombay for distribution.

2 The funds available, however, permitted of the publication of only nine copies of this work. They were distributed to the India Office, the British Museum, the Royal Asiatic Society, the Bombay Secretariat, the Bombay Branch of the Royal Asiatic Society, the Hon'ble Mr. Gibbs, C.S.I., Dr. Burgess, myself, and, I think, the Bodleian Library.

3 I am speaking, of course, only of such publications as bear on the history of that part of the country which is the subject of the present paper. Many other inscriptions were published by other scholars in the same Journals, and in the *Asiatic Researches* and the *Journal of the Asiatic Society of Bengal*.

the inscriptions included in Major Dixon's collection, and of some others collected by himself.

It is from the sources indicated above, and from such other unpublished inscriptions as I myself have collected and have in hand for publication, that the materials for the present paper have been drawn.

To a certain extent the ancient history of the country can be at present treated only as the history of the dynasties that successively ruled over it. The subordinate governments, the different territorial divisions and the changes that they underwent, the decay of the Buddhist and Jain religions, the spread of the Saiva faith, especially in its form of Lingáyatism, and similar topics, still remain to be worked out in detail. The dominions of the dynasties treated of in this paper extended sometimes to the north as far as the Vindhya mountains and the Narmadá river, sometimes to the east as far as the shores of the sea of Bengal, and usually to the south for a considerable distance into Maisur. They, therefore, were not always confined to the Kanarese districts of the Bombay Presidency. But they did always include those districts; and the chief seats of government were always within, or close to the borders of, them. The history of the dynasties, therefore, with notices of the localities in which their inscriptions are found and over which accordingly their sway extended, and with such other details as have as yet been worked out, gives, as far as we can as yet decipher it, the history of the districts.

In official language, three out of the four Kanarese districts of this Presidency, *viz.* the Belgaum, Kaládgi, and Dhárwád Collectorates, are, together with the Kolhápur, Miraj, and other Native States, always called the 'Southern Maráthá Country.' A more complete misnomer, however it originated, could not well have been devised. It is true that, in one of the earliest inscriptions, of Pulikesi II., this part of the country is included in what was known then, and even many centuries before his time,[1] as Maháráshtra, or 'the great country.' But the word had originally, and in his time, a signification very different from the special meaning which its corruption, 'Maráthá', carries now, and denoted simply the great and comparatively unknown region lying to the south of the early A'ryan settlements in Hindustán. In the whole area of the country treated of in this paper, not a single Maráthi inscription has been discovered of a greater age than two or three centuries. With the exception that a few Prákrit words occur here and there, the inscriptions are all either in pure Sanskrit or pure Kanarese, or in the two languages combined. This fact speaks of itself as to what was the vernacular of the country in early times. In the present day, the people and the language of the British districts are Kanarese; and the Kanarese people and language have been displaced, to a certain

---

1 It is mentioned, as 'Maháratha,' twice in the *Mahávamso*, Chap. XII., pp. 71 and 74; I owe this reference to the kindness of Professor Weber.—The passage refers to the deputation of the Buddhist *Thero* Mahá-Dharmarakshita to Mahárashtra, in the third century B.C. At the same time, the *Thero* Rakshita was deputed to Waniwási or Banawási in North Kanara, and the *Thero* Mahádeva to Mahishamandala or Maisur. See *Ind. Ant.*, Vol. III., p. 273.

extent, by the Maráthi people and language in the Native States, only because those States were established by the aggressions of Maráthás from the north, whose local influence proved to be greater than that of the native rulers whom they dispossessed. Even in those Native States, and in Maráthi official correspondence, the Political Agent at Kolhápur is to the present day always addressed as the Political Agent, not of the 'Dakshina-Mahárásbtra,' or 'Southern Maráthá Country,' but of the 'Karavira Ilákhá and the Karnátaka Pránt'.

SECTION II.

THE EARLY DYNASTIES.

The earliest inscription that has as yet been found is one in the Páli language, engraved on the two edges of a large slate slab, on which was carved a five-hooded cobra, in the court of the great temple at Banawási in North Kanara.[1] It is not dated in the Saka or any other definite era; but it is undoubtedly very early, and is allotted by Pandit Bhagwánlál Indraji to the second century A.D. It is of the time of a king named Háritiputra-Sátakarni of the Vinhukadadutu family or, perhaps, of the Dutu family of the place called Vinhukada or Vishnukata. Who this Háritiputra was, has not yet been determined.[2] His title of Sátakarni, being associated with the Andhrabhritya dynasty, suggests that in very early times the country round Banawási may have belonged to the Andhrabhritya kings; but it has not been yet shown that the title did not belong to other dynasties also. To whatever dynasty, however, this king may have belonged, it seems not improbable that he is the Sátakarni, lord of Dakshinápatha or 'the region of the south', whom the *Mahákshatrapa* Rudradámá, the son of Chashtana, of the Sáha dynasty, "without treachery twice completely conquered, but, on account of their near connection, did not completely destroy, and thus obtained glory."[3]

The first inscription, however, that gives us any extensive insight into the early history of these parts is a stone-tablet at the Meguti temple at Aihole,[4] the ancient Ayyávole or A'ryapura, in the

---

1 No. 10, p. 100, of the separate pamphlets of the Archæological Survey of Western India.

2 The Kadambas also, and the Early, Western, and Eastern Chalukyas, were Háritiputras, or 'of the sons of Háriti.' The name is not explained by the myth given in the later Western Chálukya inscriptions,—if only for the reason that Hâriti is there the name of a man; whereas in the Háritiputra of the early inscriptions the vowel of the last syllable is long, *i.e.* Háriti is the name of a woman, not of a man. The name Háritiputra is, in fact, exactly analogous to the Gautamiputra, Vásishthiputra, and Mádhariputra, which were names of respectively two of the Sátakarnis, of Pulumáyi, and of Purushadatta, of the Andhrabhritya dynasty. And it is curious that we find Háritiputra occurring in the above inscription as the name of a king who may himself have belonged to the Andhrabhritya dynasty, and who was ruling over that part of the country in which the Kadambas subsequently appeared, and in which they were succeeded by the Chalukyas. The Chalukyas, however, had this name of Háritiputra even when they were in the north; as is shown by the Kaira grant of Vijayarája or Vijayavarmá, the earliest of their inscriptions as yet discovered. And that the same name,—though whether as belonging to a king, or to a private person, is not certain,—was known elsewhere in the north in early times, is shown by an inscription at Riwá in the Allahábád neighbourhood; it records the construction of a cave by Háritiputra-Saunaka, and is evidently of very early date, being referred by Dr. Hoernle to about B.C. 200, though Dr. Burgess considers that it is of somewhat later date (*Ind. Ant.*, Vol. IX., p. 121.)

3 Junágad inscription; *Second Archæological Report*, pp. 128 &c.

4 The 'Iwullee' of the maps, Lat. 16° 1' N., Long. 75° 67' E., in the Hungund Táluká.

Kaládgi District. It is of the time of the Western Chalukya king Pulikesi II., and is dated Saka 556 (A.D. 634-5).[1] From it we learn that, at the time of the advent of the Chalukyas, the dominant families in this part of the country, whom one by one the Chalukyas subjugated and dispossessed, were the Nalas, the Mauryas, the Kadambas, the Mátangas, and the Katachchuris; and that they came more or less in hostile contact at the same time with the Gangas, the A'lupas, and the Pallavas of Kánchi or Conjeveram. Other opponents of the Chalukyas are mentioned in the same inscription,—A'ppáyika-Govinda, who was probably of the Ráshtrakuta family, the Látas, the Málavas, the Gurjaras, Harsha or Harshavardhana of Kanyákubja, the Kosalas, the Kalingas, the Cholas, the Keralas, and the Pándyas; but they are mentioned in connection with the more extended conquests of Pulikesi II. to the north, the east, and the south, after the consolidation of the Western Chalukya power at Vátápi or Bádámi,[2] and consequently no further account of them is called for in the present paper.

The Nalas, and the Mauryas.

The Nalas and the Mauryas are mentioned in connection with Kirttivarmá I., who was the father of Pulikesi II., and whose reign terminated in Saka 489 (A.D. 567-8). Of the Nalas nothing more is yet known, as they are only spoken of in this inscription and in the Miraj grant of Jayasimha III.[3] And of the Mauryas, all the information that we have, furnished in the same inscriptions, is that they were a reigning family in the Konkana. As has been suggested to me by Mr. Ratirám Durgárám, B.A., it is not at all improbable that their capital was the Puri, or 'the city, the goddess of the fortunes of the western ocean,' which is mentioned in the verse immediately following that in which their subjugation is recorded, and that this is the same town as the Puri which, in the eleventh century A.D., was the capital of the Siláháras of the Konkana. These Mauryas were perhaps descendants of the Maurya dynasty of Pátaliputra, which was founded by Chandragupta, the Sandrocottus of the Greeks, in the fourth century B.C., and of descendants of which we seem to have some still more recent traces in Western India, in the twelfth and thirteenth centuries A.D., in the *Mahámandalesvaras* or great feudatory nobles of the Gutta family, or the lineage of Chandragupta, whose inscriptions[4] are found at and in the neighbourhood of Chaudadámpur in

---

1 *Third Archæological Report*, p. 129; and *Indian Antiquary*, Vol. VIII., p. 237.

2 For this identification, see the papers referred to in note 1 above. Bádámi is the chief town of the Táluká of the same name in the Kaládgi District, and is in Lat. 15° 55′ N., and Long. 75° 45′ E.

3 *Ind. Ant.*, Vol. VIII., p. 10.

4 The inscriptions at present available do not afford materials sufficient for a separate chapter on the Gutta *Mahámandalesvaras*. It will, therefore, be useful to collate here whatever is known about them.—The family is called sometimes the Guttakula, and sometimes the Chandraguptavamsa, Chandraguptánvaya, or Chandraguptamahárájádhirájakula; and it is deduced from, or through, the great Vikramáditya, king of Ujjayini in Málava, whom one of the inscriptions (*Páli, Sanskrit, and Old-Canarese Inscriptions*, No. 109) appears to represent as a descendant of Chandragupta. The family is also attributed to the Somavamsa, or lineage of the moon. The members of it all had the family-title of *Ujjayani-puravar-ádhisvara*, or *Ujjeni-puravar-ádhisvara*, 'supreme lord of Ujjayani, the best of cities,'—and, in one instance (*P. S. and O.-C. Inscriptions*, No. 108) also of *Pátali-puravar-ádhisvara*, or 'supreme lord of Pátali, the best of cities', which was the city of Chandragupta. They also had the title of *Pannirbara-ganda*, or 'the punisher of the Twelve'; but the meaning of

the Dhárwád District and at Halebid in Maisur, and who were feudatories of the Western Chálukya kings and their successors.

The Kadambas.

The Kadambas are first mentioned in connection with the same monarch, Kirttivarmá I. Two later families,—called, with a slight difference in the first syllable of the name, Kádambas; and, though they pretend to great antiquity, probably not the direct descendants of the original Kadamba stock,—will be noticed further on, in Sections XI. and XII. But we are concerned here only with the early Kadambas of Palásiká or Halsi,[1] in the Belgaum District, and of Vaijayanti or Banawási,[2] in North Kanara. They are known from

---

this is not quite clear, though it appears to refer to the conquest of twelve *Mándalikas* or *Mandalesvaras* who attacked them. And they carried the banners of a sacred fig-tree and of Garuda, and used the mark or signet of a lion. Their family-god was Siva, under the name of Mahákála of Ujjayini.—And we have the following specific names and dates:—1, Either Govinda, the *Mahápradhána* and *Dandanáyaka* of the Western Chálukya king Vikramáditya VI., who had the government of the Banavåse Twelve-thousand province, was of the Gutta family, or some member of that family held office under Govinda; but the photograph of this inscription being incomplete, this point cannot at present be cleared up (*P. S. and O.-C. Inscriptions*, No. 108);—2, An inscription of the Kalachuri king Sankama, dated Saka 1101 (A.D. 1179-80), the Vikári *samvatsara*, mentions a *Mahámandalesvara* of the Gupta family whose name seems to be Sampakara, but the photograph is rather indistinct (*P. S. and O.-C. Inscriptions*, No. 183);—3, In Saka 1103 (A.D. 1181-2), the Plava *samvatsara*, one of the feudatories of the Kalachuri king A'havamalla was the *Mahámandalesvara* Vikramáditya of the Gutta family, who was governing at the city of Guttavolal; this place may be either the modern Guttal, near Chaudadámpur, in the Karajgi Táluká of the Dhárwád District, or the modern Holal, in the Ballári District, about six miles to the east of Guttal, and on the opposite bank of the Tungabhadrá river (*P. S. and O.-C. Inscriptions*, No. 230);—4, In Saka 1109 (A.D. 1187-8), the Plavamga *samvatsara*, in Saka 1113 (A.D. 1191-92), the Virodhikrit *samvatsara*, and in Saka 1135 (A.D. 1213-14), the Srimukha *samvatsara*, the same *Mahámandalesvara* Vikramáditya was governing the Banavåse Twelve-thousand province at his capital of Guttavolal; and, as these three inscriptions mention the name of no paramount sovereign, he seems to have been then independent (*P. S. and O.-C. Inscriptions*, No. 231, 109, and 234);—5, An inscription of the Devagiri-Yádava king Singhana II., of Saka 1159 (A.D. 1237-38), the Hemalambi *samvatsara*, mentions the *Mahámandalesvara* Joyideva of the Gutta family, with whose permission a grant was made, in the neighbourhood of Guttal, by one Chikkadeva, an official of Singhana II. (unpublished);—and 6, In Saka 1184 (A.D. 1262-63), the Dundubhi *samvatsara*, one of the feudatories of the Devagiri-Yádava king Mahádeva was the *Mahámandalesvara* Guttarasa of the Gutta family, who was governing at his capital of Guttavolal (*P. S. and O.-C. Inscriptions*, Nos. 110 and 111).

1 Lat. 15° 32′ N., Long. 74° 40′ E., in the Khánápur Táluká.

2 Lat. 14° 33′ N., Long. 75° 5′ E., in the Sirsi Táluká.—Banawási is a place of very considerable antiquity. It is the Waniwási to which, as recorded in the *Mahávamso*, the Buddhist *Thero* Rakshita was deputed, in the third century B.C., shortly after the great council held at Pátaliputra in the eighteenth year of Asoka (*Ind. Ant.*, Vol. III., p. 273). It is also mentioned, in the second century A.D., under the name of Banaausa, Banaosa, or Banauasi, by Ptolemy, in whose map it is entered to the east by south from Barugaza or Broach. In inscriptions, the earliest mention of it, under the name of Vanavási, is in the Aihole Meguti inscription. In the later inscriptions, the name is written Banavási in Sanskrit passages, and Banavåse and Banavase in Kanarese passages.—Mr. Kittel considers that the etymology is *bana*, *vana*, 'forest, wood,' + the Kanarese *base*, *basi*, 'spring of water,' and that Vanavási is only the Sanskritised form of the original Drávidian name (*Nágavarmá's Canarese Prosody*, Introd., p. 31, note). But the occurrence of the form Banavåse points rather to this being the first form of the name, and to its being a corruption of an original Sanskrit form Vanavása, 'the residence or settlement in the forests.' Taking the name as an original Sanskrit one, Vanavási would be the *pura* or 'city' of the *mandala* or 'province' of Vanavása. This is in accordance with the inscriptions. The Vanavási of the Aihole inscription is plainly the city, not the province. And in the later inscriptions, the form Banavási is always coupled with the word *pura* (*e.g.*, *Ind. Ant.*, Vol. X., p. 252, l. 24), while the forms Banavåse and Banavase are always coupled either with the word *nád*, 'district, province,' (*e.g.*, *P. S. and O.-C. Inscriptions*, No. 178, l. 34), or with the word *pannichchásira*, 'twelve thousand,'

ten copper-plate grants, of which seven were found at Halsi,[1] and three at Devagiri[2] in the Dhárwád District. Their principal capital was Palásiká; but Vaijayanti[3] also was one of the seats of their

---

(*e.g.*, *Ind. Ant.*, Vol. X., p. 252, l. 30-31), that being the number of villages of which the province consisted; the only exceptions are, on the one hand, the *Vanavásapura* of *P. S.* and *O.-C. Inscriptions*, No. 178, l. 33, where the use of the form Vanavása is required by the metre, and, on the other hand, the *Banavásipannichchásira* and the *Banavásimandala* of the Ráshtrakuta inscriptions in the Hángal Táluká and of *P. S.* and *O.-C. Inscriptions*, No. 120, ll. 31 and 34, and the *Vanavásimandala* of the Harihar grant of Vinayáditya. So, also, in the *Vikramánkadevacharita* (Bühler's edition, V., 23, and XIV., 4; see also *Ind. Ant.*, Vol. V., pp. 320 and 321), the *mandala* is called Vanavása; the city itself does not seem to be mentioned in this poem.—It is, perhaps, rather a hazardous conjecture to make; but it appears to me not at all improbable that it may be shown hereafter that the Vanavása province is the part of the country in which the Pándavas spent the twelve years of their banishment to the forests, as related in the *Vana-Parva* or third book of the *Mahábhárata*. There are at least strong and ancient traditions in justification of such a conjecture. Thus, at Balagámve, eighteen miles to the south-east of Banawási, there is an inscription (*P. S. and O.-C. Inscriptions*, No. 155) which says that, after the celebration of the *Rájasuya* sacrifice, "the five Pándavas came to Balligáve and established these five *lingas*." And the town of Hángal, sixteen miles to the north-east of Banawási, is called in the inscriptions (*P. S. and O.-C. Inscriptions*, No. 123, ll. 25 and 33, No. 178, l. 33, and other passages to be published hereafter) Virátakote and Virátanagari, 'the fort or city of Viráta,' Viráta being the name of the king at whose court the Pándavas spent the thirteenth year of their exile, and whose daughter Uttará was married to Arjuna's son Abhimanyu, as related in the *Viráta-Parva* or fourth book of the *Mahábhárata*.—Sir Walter Elliot has shown that the tradition, that Hángal is the place where the Pándavas resided during their exile from Indraprastha or Delhi, is even still current among the inhabitants (*Ind. Ant.*, Vol. V., p. 179).

1 *Ind. Ant.*, Vol. VI., p. 22 &c.; and *P. S. and O.-C. Inscriptions*, Nos. 2, and 5 to 10.

2 *Ind. Ant.*, Vol. VII., p. 33 &c.; and *P. S. and O.-C. Inscriptions*, Nos. 1, 3 and 4. This Devagiri is in Lat. 14° 51′ N., and Long. 75° 26′ E., in the Karajgi Táluká.

3 In No. 10, p. 28, note 2, of the separate pamphlets of the Archæological Survey of Western India, Dr. Bühler quotes the St. Petersburg Dictionary to the effect that Vaijayanti occurs in both Bráhmanical and Jain books as the name of a town on the coast of the Konkan, and suggests that "it is probably the Greek Byzantion."—The similarity of the names of Vaijayanti and Buzantion is, of course, very tempting. But this identification cannot be accepted, if it is to be held that Buzantion was, without doubt, on the coast.—The name of Vaijayanti has not as yet been met with in inscriptions found at Banawási itself. But the name of Jayantipura does occur in inscriptions at that place,—notably in one, given by me in the *Ind. Ant.*, Vol. IV., p. 207, which records that the *mancha* or stône cot of the idol of the temple of Madhukesvara at Banawási was presented to that idol, *at the city of Jayantipura*, by a certain Raghunáyaka of Sodá, or Sundá in North Kanara,—and in many other inscriptions in that neighbourhood; and there is no doubt whatever that Jayantipura was Banawási.—As regards Vaijayanti, the Kadamba inscriptions do not give any indication as to where this place was. But the Sorab copper-plate inscription of the Western Chalukya king Vinayáditya, dated Saka 614 or A.D. 692-3 (*P. S. and O.-C. Inscriptions*, No. 16), records a grant of the village of Sáthivoge in the Edevolal *vishaya* or district, to the north-east of the city of Vaijayanti. The original runs *Sri-Vaijayanti-puro......................purvvottara-vi*[*di**]*sáyám Edevolal-náma-vishaye*. Between *puro* and *purvvottara* there are three letters which are very indistinct in the photograph; the passage may be read *puro dakshina-purvvottara*, or, which seems more probably correct, *pur-opakanthe purvvottara*; at any rate it suffices to show that part, at least, of the Edevolal district lay to the north-east of Vaijayanti. This district is mentioned again in the Harihar grant of the same king, dated Saka 616 (*Ind. Ant.*, Vol. VII., p. 300), which records a grant of the village of Kiru-Kágámási in the Edevolal *bhoga* in the Vanavási *mandala* or province. Also a Ráshtrakuta inscription at Kyásanur, dated Saka 868 for 867, states that the Edevolal district was in the Banavási *nád* or province. And, in the twelfth and thirteenth centuries A.D., Edevolal was still the name of a *kampana* or sub-division, containing seventy villages, of the Pánungal or Hángal Five-hundred, which was one of the divisions of the Banavási Twelve-thousand: and the inscriptions show that it included Kyásanur, seven miles to the south-west of Hángal; Gejjihalli, two miles to the south of Hángal; A'lur and Bálur, each about three miles to the south by east from Hángal; Araleswar, about three miles to the east by north from Hángal; and

power, and Uchchasringi[1] was another; and still another is mentioned, Triparvata, which has not as yet been identified. The Halsi grants give us the following names:—

Kákusthavarma.

Sántivarmá. (Not named.)

Mrigesavarmá. (Not named.)

Ravivarmá, Bhánuvarmá. Sivaratha.

Harivarmá.

And the Devagiri grants, in addition to mentioning Mrigesavarmá, give us the names of Krishnavarmá and his son Devavarmá, who may have been either anterior to Kákusthavarmá, or slightly subsequent to Harivarmá, there being nothing in the inscriptions to decide the point either way. These Kadambas were of the Jain religion, and belonged to the Mánavya *gotra* and were 'of the sons of Háriti'.[2] They seem to have established their power originally by defeating either the Ganga or the Pallava kings, or both combined. Subsequently, Mrigesavarmá again conquered both of them. And Ravivarmá established himself, and re-established his family, at Palásiká, by overthrowing Chandadanda, the lord of Kánchi, who was undoubtedly of the Pallava dynasty. The precise date of the Kadambas is not known; for, with one exception, their grants are dated, when at all, only in the years of their reigns. The sole exception is the grant of Kákusthavarmá, which is dated in the eightieth year of victory; and here, unfortunately, we have no information as to the victory from

---

Yelawatti, about six miles to the north of Hángal.—Hángal is sixty-four miles distant, to the north-east, from the coast; and the only place of ancient importance on the coast, in an approximate south-west direction from Hángal, is Honáwar in North Kanara. Honáwar has already been identified with the Naoura of the *Periplus of the Erythræan Sea* (*Ind. Ant.*, Vol. VIII., p. 145). Even if it had not been thus disposed of, it does not lie within the limits of the Vanavási province, which did not extend below the Western Ghauts. And, even if it had lain within the limits of that province, it would hardly,—with sixty-four miles of country, including the Ghauts, intervening,—have been selected to give the direction of a small inland district which, being close to, and on the further side of, the capital of the province of which it formed a part, would naturally have its position defined with reference to that capital. And, finally, if, as I expect, the real reading of the Sorab plates is *upakanthe*, 'in the proximity of,'—(I have made several attempts to get the original plates for perusal, but without success),—this expression entirely excludes the possibility of there being a reference to any place so far away as the coast.—Banawási is only sixteen miles from Hángal, and approximately to the south-west. And it is the only large town in the Vanavási province which could suitably be selected for laying down the bearing of the Edevolal district, in the way in which it is laid down in the Sorab inscription. I think, therefore, that, on all the facts combined, it must be taken as clearly established that Vaijayanti, as well as Jayantipura, was a name of Banawási.—The seaside mart, which by the Greeks was called Buzantion, is usually identified with Vijayadurg in the Ratnágiri District, about one hundred and seventy miles to the north-west from Hángal.

1 Uchchangidurga near Harihar, Lat. 14° 34′ N., Long. 76° 7′ E.; Mr. Rice, *Mysore Inscriptions*, p. xxxix.

2 *Háritiputra*; see p. 5, note 2.

the date of which the computation is made. But the application of the term 'Pausha year' to the third year of Mrigesavarmá's reign, and of the term 'Vaisákha year' to the eighth year of his reign, —and the mention of the *eighth* fortnight of the rainy season in one of his grants, and of the *sixth* fortnight of the winter season in Bhánuvarmá's grant, indicating that, at the time of these grants, the primitive division of the year into three seasons only, not into six as now, was still followed, as it was followed in the Násik cave inscriptions,—probably contain the clue which will enable us hereafter to determine the date of these kings with accuracy. Meanwhile I would place the culmination of the power of the Kadambas, and the date of the above-mentioned kings, about the close of the fifth century A.D., a little anterior to the subjugation of the Kadambas by Kirttivarmá I. Mr. Rice has allotted the specific dates of A.D. 438 to Krishnavarmá, A.D. 538 to Kákusthavarmá, A.D. 570 to Mrigesavarmá, and A.D. 600 to Bhánuvarmá.[1] The bases for the last three dates are not given by him. The date of A.D. 438 for Krishnavarmá is based on the statement, in the Ganga grants, that the sister of a Kadamba king named Krishnavarmá was given in marriage to the Ganga king Mádhava II., whose reign is accepted by Mr. Rice as having ended in A.D. 425. But, as I cannot agree with Mr. Rice in his opinion of the authenticity of these Ganga grants, therefore I cannot concur with him in thus arriving at a specific date for Krishnavarmá. One of the Kadamba inscriptions mentions incidentally another early dynasty, that of the Sendrakas, the representative of which, in the time of the Kadamba king Harivarmá, was Bhánusakti. But all else that we at present know for certain about this dynasty is that, in the time of the Western Chalukya king Vikramáditya I., the representative of it was Devasakti who seems to have been a feudatory of the Chalukya monarch,[2] and that, in the time of Vinayáditya, the son of Vikramáditya I., the representative of it was Pogilli, who, again, appears to have been a feudatory of the Chalukyas.[3]

The Sendrakas.

The Mátangas, and the Katachchuris.

The Mátangas and the Katachchuris are mentioned in connection with Mangalisa, who was the younger brother and successor of Kirttivarmá I., and whose reign commenced in Saka 489 (A.D. 567-8) and terminated in the early part of Saka 532 (A.D. 610-1). Of the Mátangas nothing is known, except this mention of them. But *mátanga* means 'a Chándála, a man of the lowest caste an outcaste, a Kiráta mountaineer, a barbarian;' and the Mádigas, *i.e.* the Mahángs of this part of the country, usually call themselves Mátangi-makkalu, *i.e.* 'the children of Mátangi or Durgá,' who is their goddess. It is probable, therefore, that the Mátangas of this inscription were some aboriginal family of but little real power, and not of sufficient importance to have left any records of themselves. As regards the Katachchuris of this inscription,—whether this form of the name is due only to a mistake of the engraver, or whether it is a genuine and authentic variety,[4] —those who are really meant are

---

1 *Mysore Inscriptions*, p. xxxvii. 2 *Ind. Ant.*, Vol. X., p. 244.
3 *P. S. and O.-C. Inscriptions*, No. 152.
4 The *t* of Katachchuri is the cerebral *t*, usually expressed by a dot under it; and the *l* of Kalachuri is the second form of *l*, usually transliterated by a dot under

undoubtedly the predecessors of the Kalachuris of later times; and in the description of Mangalisa in the Miraj grant,[1] the word used is Kálachchuri (by a metrical license for Kalachuri), and not Katachchuri. The later Kalachuris will be noticed further on in this paper; but nothing more is known at present in respect of their ancestors of the time of Mangalisa, except that the Buddharája, son of Samkaragana, whom he is said in two of his inscriptions to have conquered, very probably was, as General Cunningham has suggested,[2] an early king of this dynasty. This, in fact, seems to be rendered almost certain by the Mahákuta column inscription of Mangalisa, which, after mentioning the conquest of king Buddha and the seizure of his riches, records that the wealth of the Kalatsuris (evidently a Sanskritised form of Kalachuri) was given to the temple of Makutesvara.

The Gangas.

The Gangas are mentioned in connection with Pulikesi II., who succeeded to the throne in Saka 532 (A.D. 610-1) and continued to reign up to at least Saka 556. Any detailed notice of them is not called for in this paper, as their dominions lay in what is now the territory of Maisur, and it was only in the extreme south and south-east parts of what is now the Bombay Presidency that the Chalukyas came in contact with them. Previous to that they had been conquered by Mrigesa. of the Kadamba dynasty of Palásiká.[3] Seven Ganga copper-plate grants have been published by Mr. Rice,[4] and one by myself,[5] and three stone-tablet inscriptions by Mr. Kittel;[6] and such information concerning this dynasty as is derivable from them and from an old Tamil chronicle called the *Kongudesarájakal* has been already compiled and published by Mr. Rice,[7] and the result is a tolerably lengthy account and list of kings, such as it is. There was undoubtedly an early and important dynasty of Ganga kings; for, in addition to the present inscription, it is mentioned, as has been indicated, also in one of the Kadamba grants of Mrigesavarmá. But, while of necessity I admit this much, I cannot go further than this; and, especially I cannot say with Mr. Rice that "the true history of this important line of kings may be said to have been entirely brought to light and authenticated by the inscriptions" mentioned above. If these inscriptions could be accepted as genuine, they would certainly establish Mr. Rice's point. But,—whereas the grant published by myself, belonging to the third generation inclusive of the founder of the dynasty, purports to be dated in Saka 169 (A.D. 247-8), and therefore to be the oldest known record of the kind, of fixed date, in Western India,—there are incontrovertible grounds for stamping this grant at once as spurious. For, not only do the characters in which it is engraved show most conclusively that it is a forgery of not earlier than the tenth century A.D., but also the date established by it cannot

---

it. Hence Katachchuri may very easily be accepted as a genuine early form of Kalachuri.

1 *Ind. Ant.*, Vol. VIII., p. 10.

2 *Archæological Reports*, Vol. IX., p. 77.

3 *Ind. Ant.*, Vol. VI., p. 25.

4 *Id.*, Vol. I., p. 363; Vol. II., p. 155; Vol. V., pp. 133 and 138; and Vol. VII., pp. 168 and 174; and *Mysore Inscriptions*, p. 284.

5 *Id.*, Vol. VIII., p. 212.

6 *Id.*, Vol. VI., p. 99.

7 *Mysore Inscriptions*, pp. xl. &c.

possibly be made to fit in with the dates established by the other grants for subsequent generations of the same dynasty.[1] And further still, this grant of Saka 169, and the Merkara grant of the year 388, and the Nágamangala grant of Saka 698, were all engraved, on their own showing, by one and the same man, Visvakarmácharya. The other grants may all be criticised in the same way, palæographically, and on other grounds. But we have also extraneous corroborative evidence of the most important kind. These grants all agree in respect of the first three generations of the dynasty,—*viz.* Konganivarmá (or Mádhava I.), the founder of the dynasty; Mádhava II., the son and successor of Konganivarmá; and Harivarmá, the son and successor of Mádhava II.,—and the grant published by myself gives Saka 169 as the date of Harivarmá. Now amongst the numerous stone-tablets extant at Lakshmeswar within the limits of the Dhárwád District, there is one of the Ganga dynasty[2] which gives exactly the same account of these three generations,—adding also Mádhava I. as the proper name of Konganivarmá, the latter being really only a family-title,—and records a grant by Márasimha, the younger brother of Harivarmá, in Saka 890 (A.D. 968-9). If the Lakshmeswar inscription were a forgery, the forgers of it would certainly have given it a much earlier date than Saka 890, and would probably have endeavoured to imitate the more ancient characters, instead of engraving it in genuine characters of the tenth century A. D. Taking all things into consideration,—the palæographical and other objections to, and the internal inconsistencies in, the copper-plate grants; the existence of this stone-tablet at Lakshmeswar; and, Márasimha having also had the title of Satyavákya, the probability that Mr. Kittel's Kiggatnád stone-tablet inscription[3] of Satyavákya-Kongunivarmá, dated Saka 900 (A.D. 978-9), is another inscription of Márasimha,[4]—there can be no doubt whatever that the dates of the copper-plate grants are spurious, and that the date of the Lakshmeswar stone-tablet inscription is the true one for the third generation from the founder of the dynasty. And, finally, if any further argument is required, there is one more point which is of the most conclusive kind. I have just seen the advanced proofs of a paper by Mr. Rice on the Ráshtrakuta kings, in which he draws attention to the fact, which I had overlooked, that the Merkara plates mention a king named Akálavarsha, —undoubtedly a Ráshtrakuta, as Mr. Rice urges,—the grant, in fact, purporting to be made by a minister of this Akálavarsha with the sanction of the Ganga king.[5] As will be seen further on, the tradition of the Miraj plates of the eleventh century A.D. mentions

---

1 The Merkara plates purport to record a grant in the year 388, which can be only Saka 388, by the great grandson of the Harivarmá of the grant of Saka 169. And the Nágamangala plates purport to record a grant in Saka 698 by the eleventh or twelfth in succession to Harivarmá.

2 *Ind. Ant.*, Vol. VII., p. 101; also see p. 112.

3 *Id.*, Vol. VI., p. 102.

4 See *Id.*, Vol. VII., p. 103.

5 Mr. Rice considers that he was the *exiled* minister of Akálavarsha. I should prefer the equally justifiable hypothesis that he *had been* the minister of Akálavarsha, and that, either on the death of that king he voluntarily or compulsorily left the Ráshtrakutas and took service under the other dynasty, or, on the subversion of the power of the Ráshtrakutas by the Western Chálukyas, part of their dominions, of which this minister was still in charge, fell into the possession of the Gangas.

a Ráshtrakuta king named Krishna, whose son Indra was conquered by the Early Chalukya king Jayasimha I. about the beginning of the fifth century A.D. And confirmatory evidence,—at any rate of the existence of an early king named Krishna, who would be slightly anterior in date to Jayasimha I., and who very possibly did belong to the Ráshtrakuta dynasty,—is afforded by some silver coins, found at Devaláná in the Násik District, which have the name of Krishnarája on them, and which, on palæographical grounds, are to be referred, as was done by Dr. Bhau Dáji, to the end of the fourth century A.D. The date of Jayasimha I. was, as has been said, about the commencement of the fifth century A.D.; and accordingly General Cunningham has referred these coins specifically to the king Krishna, said to belong to the Ráshtrakuta dynasty, whose son was vanquished by Jayasimha I. Now, Krishna II. of the Ráshtrakuta dynasty, for whom we have the dates of Saka 797 (A.D. 875-6) and 833 (A.D. 911-2), and also Krishna IV. of the same dynasty, for whom we have the dates of Saka 867 (A.D. 945-6) and 878 (A.D. 956-7), both had the title of Akálavarsha. And Mr. Rice,—starting with the suggestion that the fact, that nearly all the Govindas, and only the Govindas, among the Ráshtrakutas had the title of Prabhutavarsha, leads to the inference that the relations between the peculiar titles and certain names of the kings of that line were constant,—proceeds to point out that, on this analogy, Akálavarsha would indicate a king Krishna, and finally intimates that the Akálavarsha of the Merkara grant is to be identified with the king Krishna whose son was conquered by Jayasimha I. This identification, if it could be accepted, would of course be a strong argument in favour of the genuine antiquity of the Merkara plates. The full facts, however, really tend very emphatically in quite the opposite direction. Even if any such constant relation between the names and titles of the Ráshtrakuta kings, as Mr. Rice has suggested, could be established, it would still be unsafe to be positive in allotting the title of Akálavarsha to this early king Krishna, about whom we as yet know so little. But no such constant relation can be established. To take first the case of the Govindas, relied upon as the basis of his argument by Mr. Rice,—the inscriptions have given no secondary titles of Govinda I., and have given only that of Vallabha II. for Govinda II.; and, though Govinda III. and Govinda IV. certainly both had the title of Prabhutavarsha,—the former of them having also three other hereditary titles,—yet Govinda V. had not that title, but was called Suvarnavarsha II. and Vallabhanarendra II. Again, Suvarnavarsha I. was the title of Karka or Kakka II.; while Karka or Kakka III. had not that title, but had the titles of Amoghavarsha III. and Vallabhanarendra III. And finally,—to come to the Krishnas,—the only titles recorded of Krishna I. and Krishna II. are respectively Vallabha I. and Akalavarsha I.; the inscriptions mention no other names of Krishna III.; and, though Krishna IV. again had the title of Akalavarsha II., yet he had also that of Nirupama II., which had belonged in the first instance to Dhruva. These facts are quite enough to show that there was no constant relation between the names and the titles of the Ráshtrakuta kings. And, turning to another dynasty, that of the Western Chálukyas, there, also, we find that there was anything but a constant relation between the names of the kings and their titles :—the title of A'havamalla belonged to Taila II. and Somesvara I.; the title of Tribhuvanamalla belonged to Vikramáditya V. and Vikramáditya VI., but also to Somesvara IV.; and the title of Trailokyamalla belonged to Somesvara I., Jayasimha IV., and Taila III. This part of the argument, therefore, falls entirely to the ground. And,—since the alphabet of the Merkara plates is, in spite of certain attempts to reproduce the more ancient forms, certainly not earlier than the end of the ninth century A.D.; and since, other circumstances also fitting in, we have an Akálavarsha of the Ráshtrakuta dynasty whose reign lay about the middle of the tenth century A.D., and whose dominions extended at any rate to the confines of Maisur,—the obvious and the only tenable identification is that the Akálavarsha of the Merkara plates is, not the early king Krishna of the end of the fourth century A. D., but this same Akálavarsha II. or Krishna IV. of Saka 867 (A.D. 945-6) and 878 (A.D. 956-7). This disposes finally of the pretensions to antiquity of the Merkara plates. It follows, therefore, that Mr. Rice's Ganga kings are not the ones with whom the Kadambas and Pulikesi II. came in contact; and we have still to discover who the latter were, and to ascertain the authentic early history of the Ganga dynasty.

The A'lupas. The A'lupas are mentioned only in the present inscription,—apparently under the name of A'luvas, in a grant of Vinayáditya dated Saka 616,[1]—and, under the name of A'lupas again, as the foes of the Western Chálukyas in later times, in a Kádamba inscription dated Kaliyuga 4270 (A. D. 1169-70),[2] and in the *Vikramánka-devacharita* of Bilhana.[3] Who they were, and where their dominions lay, has still to be ascertained; but their kingdom must have been somewhere to the south or south-west and beyond the limits of the present Bombay Presidency.

The Pallavas. The Pallavas appear to have surpassed even the Kadambas in power and importance, and to have been certainly the most hostile and aggressive family that the Chalukyas encountered in their conquest of the Dekkan. And there plainly is something still to be explained to account for their deadly antagonism to the Chalukyas, which was of so inveterate and peculiar a character that they are called in one inscription their *natural* enemies.[4] The explanation may perhaps be found in the fact, of which General Pearse assures me, that the Pallava coins always bear the device of a bull,—intended doubtless for Nandi, as the representative of Siva. This would lead to the inference that the family-god of the Pallavas was Siva. The family-god of the Chalukyas, on the other hand, was Vishnu, and their coins and the seals of their grants always bear the device of a boar. It is possible, therefore, that the natural enmity of the Chalukyas and the Pallavas had its origin in their belonging, at least by tradition, if not by actual practice, to the two great rival forms of the Hindu religion. As Mr. Rice says, the origin of the Pallavas is as yet uncertain. But there can be but little doubt, if any, that they are the Pahlavas or Pahnavas, who, as he also points out, are mentioned in the *Puránas*, along with the Haihayas, Sakas, Yavanas, &c.; and

---

1 *Ind. Ant.*, Vol. VII., p. 300.
2 *Journal of the Bombay Branch of the Royal Asiatic Society*, Vol. IX., p. 278.
3 Buhler's edition; V., 26.
4 *Ind. Ant.*, Vol. VIII., p. 25, l. 38.

this would imply a Persian origin.[1] And, as regards the word 'Pahlav,'—which at the period of the inscriptions would naturally be represented by 'Pallava,'—Prof. Weber considers that it "became early foreign to the Persians, learned reminiscences excepted; in the Pahlavi texts themselves, for instance, it does not occur. The period when it passed over to the Indians, therefore, would have to be fixed for about the second to the fourth century A.D.; and we should have to understand by it, not directly the Persians, who are called Párasikas rather, but specially the Arsacidan Parthians."[2] In their inscriptions, however, the Pallavas claim to belong to the Bháradvája *gotra*, and therefore to be of Hindu origin. In the time of Pulikesi II., Kánchi, or Conjeveram,[3] was the central seat of their dominions. Prior to that, they had held the country of Vengi, on the eastern coast, between the rivers Krishná and Godávari, from which they were ejected by the Eastern Chalukyas at some time during the seventh century. And either their kingdom extended at the same time across India to the Western Ghauts, or, prior to their settling down in the Vengi country, their capital was Vátápi or Bádámi, as is proved by a fragmentary and ancient inscription, discovered by me not long ago at Bádámi itself.[4] Therefore, though the inscriptions as yet known do not expressly state the fact, the Chalukyas had come in contact with the Pallavas before the time of Pulikesi II., and it was from the Pallavas that they acquired Vátápi, probably in the time of Pulikesi I. The Kadamba inscriptions, also, give clear evidence of the existence of the power of the Pallavas in Western India in early times. Mrigesavarmá conquered them.[5] And Ravivarmá established himself, and re-established his family, at Palásiká, by overthrowing Chandadanda the lord of Kánchi;[6] and the Vishnuvarmá, who was slain by him, probably belonged to the same family. Also the *Senápati* Simha, of the Bháradvája *gotra*, by whose son Mrigesa a Jain temple was built at Palásiká,[7] was very possibly a member of the same family. And it seems likely that the Chandadanda, with the help of whom Pulikesi II. ejected the Mauryas from the Konkana,[8] was a descendant of the Chandadanda who was overthrown by Ravivarmá. Five early Pallava copper-plate grants have been published,—one by Mr. Foulkes,[9] and four by myself.[10] One of them is in the Prákrit language, and is probably the earliest Pallava grant that has as yet come to light; it gives the names of two kings,—Vijayaskandavarmá, and his son Vijayabuddhavarmá. Another of them mentions only one king, Attivarmá, with nothing to indicate his date or his place in the dynasty. The others establish the following short genealogy:—

---

1 *Mysore Inscriptions*, p. li.—They are mentioned in the *Vishnu-Purána*, Wilson's translation, Hall's edition, Vol. II., pp. 168, 185; and Vol. III., pp. 291, 294. And Manu (Chap. X., vv. 43, 44) says that they were a degraded division of the Kshatriya caste.

2 *History of Indian Literature*, p. 187, note 201*a*.

3 Lat. 12° 50′ N., Long. 79° 45′ E.

4 *Ind. Ant.*, Vol. IX., p. 99.

5 *Id.*, Vol. VI., p. 25.

6 *Id.*, Vol. VI., p. 30.

7 *Id.*, Vol. VI., p. 31.

8 *Id.*, Vol. VIII., p. 244.

9 *Id.*, Vol. VIII., p. 167. This one, however, is of somewhat doubtful authenticity.

10 *Id.*, Vol. V., pp. 50 and 154; and Vol. IX., pp. 100 and 102.

Skandavarmá I.
|
Víravarmá.
|
Skandavarmá II.
|
- Simhavarmá I.
  - Skandavarmá III.
    - Nandivarmá.
- Vishnugopavarmá.
  - Simhavarmá II.

Unfortunately none of these grants are dated in any era except that of the reigning king. Therefore,—though Skandavarmá I. and his successors may be safely attributed, as was done by Dr. Burnell,[1] to the fifth and sixth centuries A.D., and Vijayaskandavarmá and his son probably to a somewhat earlier time,—we are left unable to say definitely that it was any one of these kings that held Vátápi and was ejected from it by the Chalukyas. The Bádámi fragment, however, has in it the name of either Vishnu, Simhavishnu, or Narasimhavishnu; and we have a Simhavishnu and Narasimhavarmá mentioned as belonging respectively to the first and third generation of the dynasty, so far as the genealogy is given and may be relied on, in a later Pallava inscription published by Mr. Foulkes.[2]

---

1 *South-Indian Palæography*, p. 36.

2 *Ind. Ant.*, Vol. VIII., p. 273.

SECTION III.

THE EARLY CHALUKYAS.

The records that have survived of this important and powerful dynasty are so numerous, and so carefully dated in almost every instance in the well known Saka era,[1] that we enter now upon a far more definite chapter in the history of Western India. To a certain extent our knowledge of it is in outline only, simply because there has been as yet no opportunity of examining more than a very small portion of the materials already collected, and much less of investigating the other remains that exist so abundantly all over the Kanarese country, but are from year to year being wantonly destroyed or allowed through negligence to disappear. Still, such knowledge as we do possess is by no means scanty.

The accompanying table gives a complete genealogy of all the generations of this dynasty, as far as they are now known, from its first appearance in historical times down to its final extinction. The mythical account of the origin of the name Chalkya, Chalikya, and Chalukya, the etymology of which has not yet been satisfactorily explained, is that the founder of the race sprang from the spray of a water-pot (*chulka, chuluka, chaluka*), when Háriti, who wore five tufts of hair on his head, was pouring out a libation to the gods.[2] The probability is that the oldest and original form was Chalkya, and that the other forms were created by the use of

---

1 The initial date of the Saka era was the 14th March, A.D. 78; *Ind. Ant.*, Vol. VII., p. 181.

2 Handarike inscription; Elliot *MS. Collection*, Vol. I., p. 642.—The inscription, which is of the time of Vikramáditya VI., deduces the genealogy from Vishnu, through Brahmá, who was born in the water-lily that grew out of Vishnu's navel, Manu, Mándavya, and Harita, to Háriti-Panchasikha, from whose water-pot the Chalukyas sprang as stated above.—Bilhana, the *Vidyápati* or Chief Pandit of Vikramáditya VI., gives a somewhat different account, and says (*Vikramánkadeva-charita*, I., 31-58) that, when Brahmá was engaged in the morning ceremonies on the bank of the river of the gods, Indra came and represented to him that the inhabitants of the earth were becoming so indifferent about religion that it seemed as if all sacrifice to the gods would soon cease, and asked him to create a hero to destroy the enemies of religion. Brahmá turned his eyes, full of meditation, upon his water-pot, from which there then sprang forth a warrior, clothed in golden armour proof against all weapons, who was dedicated by Brahmá to the destruction of the enemies of the gods. He attained pre-eminence over all the kings of the earth; and by him there was founded a family, of which Hárita came to be considered the *ádi-pums* or 'first progenitor,' and in which Mánavya was born, who humbled the pride of his enemies.—It may be noted that the myth cannot be of very ancient invention; as,—though this derivation will suit the name of Chálukya, which only came into use on the restoration of the dynasty under Taila II., and also the name of Chaulukya, belonging only to the Anhilwád dynasty, the members of which called themselves both Chaulukyas and Chaulukikas, and the earliest date for which is the middle of the tenth century A.D.,—yet it does not suit the original name of Chalkya, Chalikya, and Chalukya.

pronunciative vowels. The Chalukyas belong originally to the Somavamsa, or lunar race; and, like the early Kadambas, they claim to belong to the Mánavya *gotra* and to be 'of the sons of Háriti'.[1] It is suggested by Mr. Rice,[2] that they borrowed these details of descent from the Kadambas, as being the most powerful and important family supplanted by them in Western India. But this can hardly be the case; for, these same details are given in the earliest known Chalukya inscription, the Khedá or Kaira grant of Vijayarája, dated Saka 394 (A.D. 472-3),[3] which was engraved before the Chalukyas left the northern part of this Presidency and, travelling southwards, came in contact with the Kadambas. The *kuladevatá*, or family-god, of the Chalukyas was Vishnu; and the principal emblem that the seals of their grants and their coins always bear is a boar, derived from one of the incarnations of Vishnu. But, in spite of this fact, in early times they displayed a considerable amount of tolerance in matters of religion, and patronised the Jain and Saiva, equally with the Vaishnava, faiths. And in the later generations they devoted themselves almost entirely to the Saiva religion, particularly in the *linga* form of worship.

The early tradition of the family is that fifty-nine kings of this dynasty reigned at Ayodhyá, and after them sixteen more over the region of the south, by which must be meant the northern part of the Dekkan immediately to the south of Ayodhyá.[4] There was then a temporary obscuration of their power, which was restored in the person of Jayasimha I.

Jayasimha I.

No inscriptions of the time of Jayasimha I., also called Jayasimharája and Jayasimhavallabha, are as yet known to exist. Should any be hereafter discovered, they will probably carry back the genealogy to still earlier times; for the directions of the Sanskrit lawyers, followed in nearly all these records, are, that the genealogical portion of the grant must give the name of at least three generations. At present the name of Jayasimha I. is the earliest historical name in this dynasty that we possess. It is given as the name of the founder of the dynasty, both in the earliest known Chalukya grant from the north, the Khedá or Kaira grant of Vijayarája mentioned above, and in the only two authentic southern inscriptions which go back to the commencement of the genealogy,—the Aihole stone-tablet of Pulikesi II., and the Miraj grant of Jayasimha III., also mentioned above. And, though I cannot speak with absolute conviction at present, I am so strongly inclined to accept the two Jayasimhas as one and the same person, that I have treated them as such in the genealogical table published herewith. None of the southern inscriptions speak of any of the royal families of the south as having been conquered by Jayasimha I., or by his son Ranarága. And,—though a grant, of the eleventh century A.D., of one of the Chola successors of the Eastern Chalukya kings, professes to tell us that, after fifty-nine emperors, commencing with Udayana, had

---

1 *Háritiputra*; see p. 5, note 2.
2 *Ind. Ant.*, Vol. VIII., p. 23; and *Mysore Inscriptions*, p. lviii.
3 *Id.*, Vol. VII., p. 241.
4 *Id.*, Vol. V., p. 17; and Vol. VIII., p. 12. See also *Vikramánkadevacharita*, I, 63.

GENEALOGY OF THE EARLY CHALUKYA, WESTERN CHALUKYA, AND WESTERN CHA'LUKYA DYNASTY.

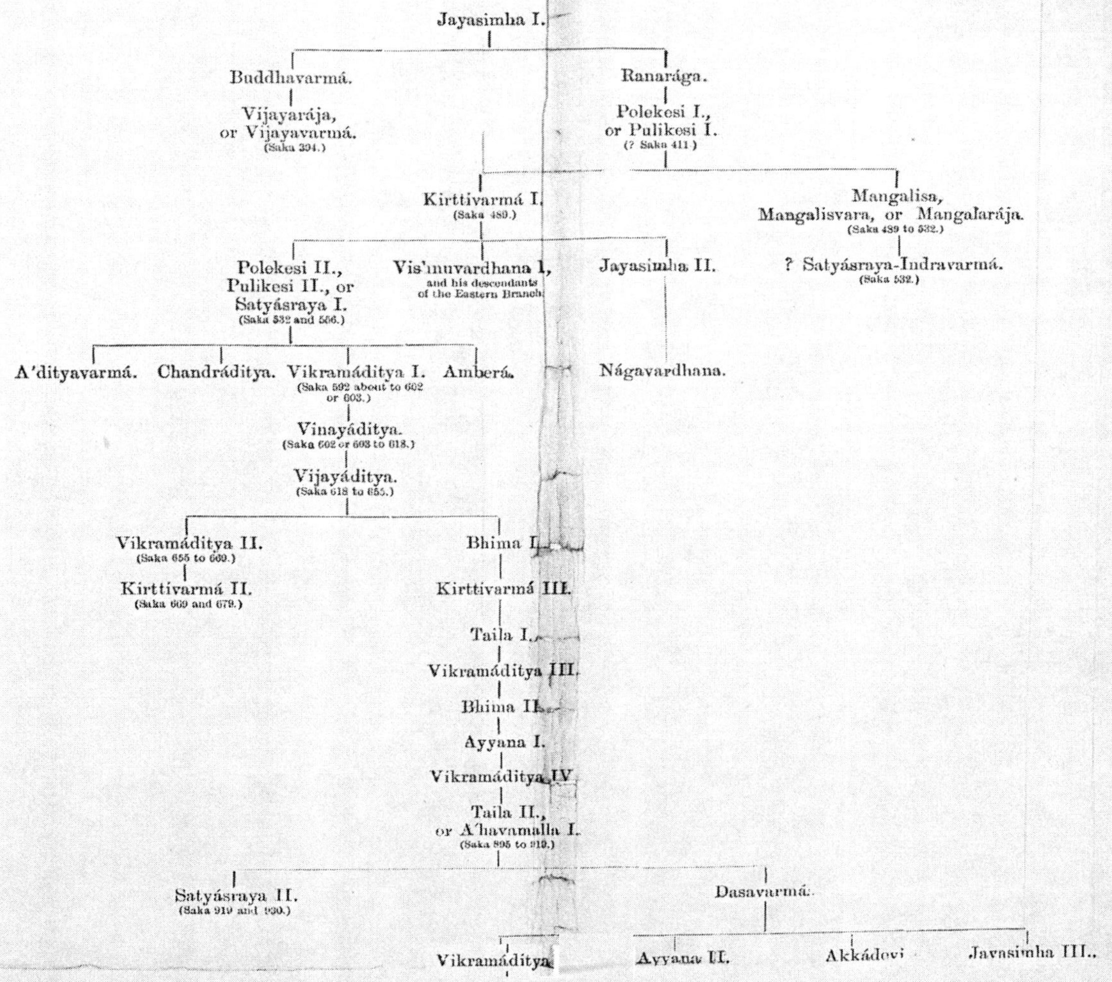

reigned in unbroken lineal succession at the city of Ayodhyá, one of his descendants, named Vijayáditya, journeyed to the south from a desire of conquest; and that, though this Vijayáditya was defeated and slain by a Pallava king named Trilochana, his son, Vishnuvardhana, married into the Pallava family; and that Vishnuvardhana's grandson Polekesivallabha, the Pulikesi II. of my table, established the Chalukya empire in the south,—still this is a mere *farrago* of vague tradition and *Puránik* myths, of no authority, based on the undoubted facts that the Chalukyas did come originally from the north and did find the Pallavas in possession of some of the territories afterwards acquired by themselves, and on a tradition of the later Kádambas that the founder of their family was named Trilochana or Trinetra.[1] If the tradition of the Miraj plates is to be accepted, it was by defeating an early Ráshtrakuta king named Indra, the son of Krishna, that Jayasimha re-established the Chalukya power after its temporary obscuration; and at that time certainly the kingdom of the Ráshtrakutas did not extend below the northern parts of the Dekkan. It may be taken as absolutely certain that Jayasimha I. had no dominion south of the Tápi or Tapti river, and perhaps not south even of the Narmadá.

Of Buddhavarmá and Ranarága, the two sons of Jayasimha I., we have no historical information, beyond the mere mention of their names. But here, again, the absence of any mention of the southern dynasties in connection with them indicates plainly that they did nothing to advance the Chalukya kingdom in that direction. Buddhavarmá, and Ranarága.

Of Vijayavarmá or Vijayarája, the son of Buddhavarmá, the only record that we have is the Kaira grant of Saka 394 (A.D. 472-3).[2] It confers the village of Pariyaya upon the priests and religious students of Jambusara, the modern Jambusar between Kaira and Broach, and is issued from the victorious camp at the city of Vijayapura. This city still remains to be identified, and has to be looked for somewhere in Gujarát. At the backs of these plates there is a cancelled grant,[3] issued at the same time and by the same king, but apparently from some other place, the name of which is only partially legible, but which may be Nándipuri, identified by Dr. Bühler with a fort of the same name just outside the Jhadeswar gate of the city of Broach.[4] Vijayavarmá.

We have no record of any descendants of Vijayarája. The next name is that of his cousin Polekesi or Pulikesi I., also called Ranavikrama or 'he who is valorous in war,' the son of Ranarága. His wife was Durlabhádevi, of the Bappura family. It was in his time that the Chalukyas left the north and invaded the south. The circumstances under which they did so are not yet clear. But the probability is that, at the death of Vijayarája, or possibly by an invasion of his kingdom which resulted in his defeat and death in battle, the power of the Chalukyas in the north was subverted, and the family expelled, by the Gurjara kings, or by the kings of Valabhi, the other most powerful rulers of those parts; and that, in his flight, directing his course to the south in the hope Pulikesi I.

---

1 *Ind. Ant.*, Vol. VII., p. 246.
2 *Id.*, Vol. VII., p. 241.
3 *Id.*, Vol. VII., p. 251.
4 *Id.*, Vol. VII., p. 62.

of finding new and unoccupied dominions there, Pulikesi I. was attended by a band of adherents sufficiently numerous and strong to enable him to eventually invade, and conquer a part of, the dominions of the Pallava king, and, by wresting the city of Vátápi from him, to establish for himself a new seat of government there. Or it is even possible that the Chalukyas were originally feudatories of the Gurjara kings, but, in the person of Pulikesi I., threw off that yoke, and, emigrating to the south, established an independent sovereignty of their own. There is no genuine inscription of the time of Pulikesi I. There is a spurious grant,[1] now in the British Museum, which purports to be of his time and to be dated Saka 411 (A.D. 489-90), and to record the building of a Jain temple and the allotment of certain grants to it at the city of Alaktakanagara in the Kuhundi district, which was governed by one of his feudatories. Saka 411 may, or may not, be within the limits of the life of Pulikesi I.; but this grant, for the reasons which I have set forth in full in my notice of it, is a forgery of not earlier than the tenth century A.D. His capital appears to have been originally Indukánti, a city which has not yet been identified, but which must be looked for somewhere in the north and possibly in the neighbourhood of Ajantá,[3] if, indeed, it does not turn out to be that place itself. It was he who first made Vátápi the capital of the Chalukyas in Western India, wresting it from the Pallavas who then held it, and established the dynasty permanently in these parts; and it is probably owing to this fact that, in the majority of the Early and Western Chalukya grants, the genealogy commences with his name. An inscription of Vikramáditya VI. at Bhárangi in Maisur, dated Saka 1039 (A.D. 1117-8),[4] seems to compare a conquest of the Chola king, who had burned Kalyána which was then the Western Chálukya capital, by Somesvara I., to a conquest of the Pallava king, and a burning of Kánchi, by Pulikesi I. This tradition, however, must be accepted with some caution, as we have no further evidence that Pulikesi I. penetrated so far into the Pallava dominions.

Kirttivarmá I.

Pulikesi I. was succeeded by his eldest son, Kirttivarmá I., who extended the Chalukya kingdom further to the south and west by defeating and subjugating the Nalas, the Mauryas, and the Kadambas. The date of his accession is not known; but his reign terminated in Saka 489 (A.D. 567-8).[5] We have as yet only one inscription of his time, and that found quite recently.[6] It is an undated Old-Kanarese inscription at A'dur, the ancient Pándipura, eight miles to the east of Hángal in the Dhárwád District; and it records that, while Kirttivarmá was reigning as supreme sovereign, and while a certain king Sinda was governing at Pándipura, endowments were made to

---

1 *Ind. Ant.*, Vol. VII., p. 209. No information is forthcoming as to where the plates were found, except that it was somewhere "in the Southern Maráthá Country or in the Karnátaka."—Alaktakanagara has not been identified. The Kuhundi or Kundi district of three thousand villages included the greater part of the Belgaum District and the Native States to the north of it, and part of the Kaládgi District.

2 *Id.*, Vol. VIII., p. 239.

3 Lat. 20° 33′ N., Long. 75° 50′ E.

4 *Elliot MS. Collection*, Vol. I., p. 557.

5 *Ind. Ant.*, Vol. X., p. 57.

6 *Ind. Ant.*, Vol. XI., p. 68.—It is the earliest known specimen of the Old Kanarese language to which a definite period can be allotted.

a Jain temple at that town. The existence of this inscription in the heart of the Kadamba territory furnishes an interesting corroboration of the statement of the Aihole Meguti inscription, that Kirttivarmá I. conquered the Kadambas.[1] It was by Kirttivarmá I. that the construction of the Vaishnava Cave, No. III., at Bádámi was originated, and probably in his reign that it was commenced.

Mangalisa.

He was succeeded by his younger brother Mangalisa, also called Mangalarája and Mangalisvara, in Saka 489. Of this king we have five inscriptions,—an undated copper-plate grant from Nerur[2] in the Sáwantwádi State;[3] an inscription, dated in the fifth year of his reign, on a large fallen column at Mahákuta near Bádámi, where there is the temple of the god Mahákutesvara, or, as the name is written in this inscription, Makutesvara;[4] an inscription on a pilaster in the verandah of the Vaishnava cave, No. III., at Bádámi, dated Saka 500 (A.D. 578-9) in the twelfth year of his reign, and recording the completion of the cave;[5] an undated inscription on the rock just outside the same cave;[6] and a copper-plate grant from the Goanese territory dated Saka 532 (A.D. 610-1),[7] in the twentieth year, not of his reign, but of his conquest of Revatidvipa,[8] which is spoken of both in the Aihole Meguti inscription and in the Miraj plates. According to the Miraj plates, he succeeded as regent during the minority of his nephew, Pulikesi II., the eldest son of Kirttivarmá I., and peaceably resigned the throne when Pulikesi II. attained maturity. But, whatever may be the circumstances under which he obtained the sceptre, the Aihole inscription speaks of a desire on the part of Mangalisa to secure the succession for his own son, and of discord and civil war between him and Pulikesi II., in the course of which he lost his life. This last occurrence must have been in the early part of Saka 532. In addition to his conquest of Revatidvipa, Mangalisa subjugated the Mátangas and the Katachchuris or Kalachuris. He seems to have acquired his kingdom in the Konkanas from a branch of the Chalukyas, otherwise unknown, settled there, the chief of whom, Svámirája, he slew. And he conquered and dispossessed another king, named Buddha, the son of Samkaragana, who very probably was, as suggested by General Cunningham,[9] of the Kalachuri dynasty. The Mahákuta column inscription, in fact, seems to render this almost certain, as, after mentioning the conquest

---

1 Bilhana does not mention the Kadambas by name in connection with the Early Chalukyas; but he says (*Vikramánkadevacharita*, I., 64) that, when they first left Ayodhyá, their conquests "in the southern region, where the betel-tree grows," extended as far as Nágarakhanda. Nágarakhanda, meaning 'the division either of the cobras or of the people of the Nága race,' was a part of the Kadamba territory, lying just to the south of A'dur, on the other side of the river Wardá. In the twelfth and thirteenth centuries A.D., Nágarakhanda was a *kampana*, or small district, containing seventy villages, part of the Banavase Twelve-thousand, and including Tiliwalli in the Hángal Táluká and Yammiganur in the Kod Táluká (Elliot *MS. Collection*, Vol. I., p. 818; and *P. S. and O.-C. Inscriptions*, No. 112).

2 Lat. 16° 1′ N., Long. 73° 42′ E.

3 *Ind. Ant.*, Vol. VII., p. 161; and *P. S. and O.-C. Inscriptions*, No. 11.

4 See *Ind. Ant.*, Vol. X., p. 102.

5 *Id.*, Vol. III., p. 305, and Vol. VI., p. 363; and *P. S. and O.-C. Inscriptions*, No. 39.

6 *Id.*, Vol. X., p. 59; and *P. S. and O.-C. Inscriptions*, No. 40.

7 *Jour. Bo. Br. R. As. Soc.*, Vol. X., p. 348.

8 *Ind. Ant.*, Vol. X., p. 57.

9 *Archæological Reports*, Vol. IX., p. 77.

of king Buddha and the seizure of his riches, it records that the wealth of the Kalatsuris (evidently a Sanskritised form of Kalachuri) was given to the temple of Makutesvara.

Satyásraya-Indravarmá.

It is recorded in the Aihole inscription that Mangalisa had a son, for whom he was desirous to secure the succession after his own death. This son's name is not given there, nor is any mention made of him in the Miraj plates. But it is just possible that he is the *Yuvarája* Satyásraya-Indravarmá or the Satyásraya-Dhruvarája-Indravarmá, the governor of Revatidvipa, by whom the grant recorded in the plates of Saka 532 from the Portuguese territory was made. That this person was at any rate in some way or other a connection of Mangalisa, is shown by his being called 'the ornament of the A'dimahábappuravamsa,'—the Bappura family being the one to which Durlabhádevi, the wife of Pulikesi I., belonged.[1] The expression applied to Satyásraya-Indravarmá may mean that his father was of the Bappura family, in which case he himself was only a connection by marriage of Mangalisa; or, as in the case of some of the titles of the later Western Chálukyas, derived from intermarriages with the Pallavas and Gangas, it may be a family-title of the Chalukyas derived from the intermarriage of Pulikesi I. with the Bappuras, or from a similar intermarriage by Mangalisa himself. However this may be, it does not appear that Mangalisa's son ever actually ascended the Chalukya throne.

---

[1] It is not yet clear, however, whether she was the mother of Mangalisa. In his inscription in which she is mentioned, he calls her, not his 'mother,' but *sva-guru-patni*, 'the wife of his own father,' which reads somewhat as if Kirttivarmá I. and Mangalisa were the sons of Pulikesi I. by different wives.

SECTION IV.

THE WESTERN CHALUKYAS.

Kirttivarmá I. left three sons,—Pulikesi II., also called Satyásraya, or 'the asylum of truth,' because 'he adhered to his promises even though they were not enforced by precept;' Vishnuvardhana I., who, being also called Kubja-Vishnuvardhana, seems to have been hump-backed; and Jayasimhavarmá or Jayasimha II., also called Jayásraya 'the asylum of victory', and Dharásraya 'the asylum of of the earth.' There was a formal division of the kingdom between the two elder brothers,—Pulikesi II. taking the western dominions, and establishing himself at Vátápi as the capital; and Vishnuvardhana I. taking the eastern dominions, and establishing himself in the Vengi country. This division must have taken place in, or very shortly after, Saka 532 (A.D. 610-1), when Mangalisa died and Pulikesi II. succeeded to the throne; and from that time forth the Western and the Eastern Branches of the Chalukya family remained separate and distinct. At the same time, Jayasimha II. appears to have received his share of the kingdom, more to the north. We are not further concerned with him; and he is known only from the undated Nirpan grant, from the Násik District, of his son Nágavardhana, also called Tribhuvanásraya, or 'the asylum of the three worlds.'[1] It is just possible that he was the progenitor of the Chaulukyas of Anhilwád, who appear historically in the tenth century A.D.[2] Nor are we any further concerned in this paper with Vishnuvardhana I. and his descendants of the Eastern Branch.

Pulikesi II., or Satyásraya I.

Polekesi or Pulikesi II., who succeeded to the throne early in Saka 532 (A.D. 610-1), was the most powerful and illustrious of the early kings of his dynasty. We have three inscriptions of his time,—a grant from Haidarábád in the Dekkan,[3] dated Saka 534 (A.D. 612-3), the third year of his reign; an undated grant from Nerur in the Sáwantwádi State;[4] and the Aihole Meguti inscription,[5] dated Saka 556 (A.D. 634-5) and Kaliyuga 3735. There is also a stone-tablet inscription at Aminbhávi in the Dhárwád District,[6] which falsely attributes to him the date of Saka 488 (A.D. 564-5); but his real date is so well known, that it is unnecessary to give any

---

1 *Ind. Ant.*, Vol. IX., p. 123.
2 *Id.*, Vol. VI., p. 180.
3 *Id.*, Vol. VI., p. 72.
4 *Id.*, Vol. VIII., p. 43.
5 *Id.*, Vol. VIII., p. 237.
6 *Elliot MS. Collection*, Vol. I., p. 672.—I have quite recently had inquiries made about the original stone, with the object of obtaining an impression of it; but, like many of the inscriptions that were in existence in Sir Walter Elliot's time, it is not now forthcoming.

reasons here for rejecting the date of this inscription.[1] His conquests were numerous and widely spread, and included the Ráshtrakutas, who invaded him under A'ppáyika-Govinda, the Kadambas of Vanavási, the Gangas, the A'lupas, the Mauryas of the Konkana, the Látas, the Málavas, the Gurjaras, the three countries known by the name of Maháráshtra and including, it is said, ninety-nine thousand villages,[2] the Kosalas, the Kalingas, the Pallavas of Kánchi, the Cholas, the Keralas, and the Pándyas. The greatest of them was his conquest of Harsha or Harshavardhana, also called Siláditya, of Kanyákubja or Kanauj, who is called, in the inscriptions, 'the warlike lord of all the region of the north.' It was by this victory that Pulikesi II. acquired the title of *Paramesvara*, or 'supreme lord,' and this, with his other name of Satyásraya, under which alone he is usually spoken of in all the later Western Chalukya inscriptions, became one of the hereditary titles of his descendants. The Chinese pilgrim Hiwen Thsang, who sojourned in India from A.D. 629 to 645, or Saka 551 to 567, visited the court of *Ho-li-sha-fa-t'an-na* or Harshavardhana, otherwise called *Shi-lo-o'-t'ie-to* or Siláditya, and describes, and apparently visited a capital of, the kingdom of *Mo-ho-la-ch'a* or Maháráshtra, the king of which was named *Pu-lo-ki-she* or Pulikesi II. His account of this kingdom is as follows:[3]—"The kingdom of *Mo-ho-la-ch'a* is nearly six thousand *li* (twelve hundred miles) in circuit. The capital, towards the west, is near a large river; its circumference is thirty *li*.[4] The soil is rich and fertile, and produces abundance of grain. The climate is warm; the manners are simple and honest. The natives are tall, and haughty and supercilious in character. Whoever does them a service may count on their gratitude; but he that offends them will not escape their revenge. If any one insult them, they will risk their lives to wipe out that affront. If one apply to them in difficulty, they will forget to care for themselves in order to flee to his assistance. When they have an injury to avenge, they never fail to give warning to their enemy; after which each puts on his cuirass and grasps his spear in his hand. In battle they pursue the fugitives, but do not slay those who give themselves up. When a general has lost a battle, instead of punishing him corporally, they make him wear women's clothes, and by that force him to sacrifice his own life. The state maintains a body of dauntless champions, to the number of several hundreds. Each time they prepare for combat, they drink wine to intoxicate them; and then one of these men, spear in hand, will defy ten thousand enemies. If they kill a man met upon the road, the law does not punish them. Whenever the army commences a campaign, these braves march in the van to the sound

---

1 See *Ind. Ant.*, Vol. V., p. 67.

2 This number may appear rather large. But the Gangavádi district, in Maisur, in the tenth and eleventh centuries A.D. included ninety-six thousand villages. *Ind. Ant.*, Vol. IV., p. 203; and *Mysore Inscriptions*, p. 209.

3 Dr. Burgess; *Ind. Ant.*, Vol. VII., p. 290.

4 Dr. Burgess has suggested that this may be Bádámi.—There is a river near Bádámi, the Malaprabhá; and about three miles to the south-east of Bádámi there is the temple of Banasamkari, which *may* be the ancient convent in which there was a stone statue of Avalokitesvara-Bodhisattva. But no traces have been found as yet of the hundred convents of Hiwen Thsang's account, or of the five *stupas* built by Asoka.

of the drum. Besides, they intoxicate many hundreds of naturally fierce elephants. At the time of their coming to blows, they drink also strong liquor. They run in a body, trampling everything under their feet. No enemy can stand before them. The king, proud of possessing these men and elephants, despises and slights the neighbouring kingdoms. He is of the race of the *Ts'a-ti-li* (Kshatriyas); his name is *Pu-lo-ki-she* (Pulikesi). His ideas are large and profound, and he extends widely his sympathy and benefactions. His subjects serve him with perfect self-devotion. At present the great king (Siláditya) carries his victorious arms from the east to the west; he subdues distant people and makes the neighbouring nations fear him: but the people of this kingdom alone have not submitted. Although he be often at the head of all the troops of the five Indies, though he has summoned the bravest generals of all the kingdoms, and though he has marched himself to punish them, he has not yet been able to vanquish their opposition. From this we may judge of their warlike habits and manners. The men love study, and follow at the same time the teachings of heresy and of truth. There are a hundred convents, which contain nearly five thousand devotees, and where they study alike the greater and lesser vehicles.[1] They reckon a hundred temples of the gods; the heretics of various sects are exceedingly numerous. Within and outside the capital, are raised five *stupas*. In all these places the four past Buddhas have sat, and, in performing their exercises, have left the marks of their feet. These monuments were constructed by king *Wu-yeu* (Asoka). There are other *stupas* in stone and brick, but they are so numerous that it would be difficult to mention all. A short distance to the south of the town, there is an ancient convent, in the middle of which is seen a stone statue of *Kwan-tseu-tasaï-p'u-sa* (Avalokitesvara-Bodhisattva). The effects of his divine power are manifested in secret: those who apply to him, obtain for the most part the objects of their vows. On the eastern frontiers of the kingdom, there is a great mountain, which shows summits heaped one upon another, chains of rocks, peaks in double rank, and scarped crests. Of old there was a convent there, which had been formed in a gloomy valley. Its lofty walls and deep halls occupied large openings in the rocks and rested against the peaks; its pavilions and its two-storied towers were backed by the caverns and looked into the valley."[2] The reputation and influence of Pulikesi II. were by no means confined to India. For, as Mr. Fergusson has shown in a paper recently read by him before the Royal Asiatic Society,[3] there is an Arabic chronicle, which records the fact that, in the thirty-sixth year of the reign of Khosru II. of Persia, presents and letters were interchanged between him and Pulikesi II. Khosru was dethroned on the 25th February A.D. 628, in the thirty-eighth year of his reign. This makes Saka 547 (A.D. 625-6), when Pulikesi II. had been about sixteen years on the throne, the date of the communication between him and the king of Persia. And in the same paper,—in fact, as the chief

---

1 The *Mahdyána* and the *Hinayána*.
2 Mr. Fergusson identifies this place with Ajantá.
3 *Jour. R. As. Soc.*, Vol. XI., p. 155.

subject of it,—Mr. Fergusson has drawn attention to a painting in one of the Ajantá caves, which depicts the presentation of a letter from a Persian king to an Indian king, who is supposed to be Pulikesi II. himself. The exact date of the termination of the reign of Pulikesi II. is not known, as none of the inscriptions of his sons, which have as yet been discovered, are dated in the Saka era, or with such details that they can be referred to the Saka era. But, as he must have been at least three years old in Saka 489, when his father, Kirttivarmá I., died, it is not likely that he continued to reign much longer after Saka 556, the date of the Aihole Meguti inscription.

After the death of Pulikesi II., the kingdom of the Western Chalukyas appears to have been invaded by the Pallavas, who succeeded in driving them for a time, on the west, back to and below the Western Ghauts, and on the south, to the Karnul District. In this the Pallavas appear to have been aided by a confederacy of the Chola and Pándya and Kerala kings.[1] And we have, perhaps, an allusion to these events in a Pallava grant of later times, published by Mr. Foulkes,[2] which compares Narasimhavarmá, one of the early Pallavas, with the saint Agastya, the destroyer of the demon Vátápi. In this comparison, it is almost impossible to avoid seeing an allusion to some early conquest of the city of Vátápi by the Pallavas.

A'dityavarmá.

Pulikesi II. had three sons, A'dityavarmá, Chandráditya, and Vikramáditya I.,[3] and a daughter, Amberá. A'dityavarmá is known from a copper-plate grant, which has only recently come to notice, from the Karnul district.[4] It is dated only in the first year of his reign, and without any reference to the Saka era. It gives no historical information, and does not expressly state that A'dityavarmá was the *eldest* of the sons of Pulikesi II. I consider this, however, to be the probability, on palæographical grounds.

Chandráditya.

Chandráditya is known only from the undated Nerur and Kochre grants of his wife, Vijayamahádevi or Vijayabhattáriká, from the Konkan.[5] They do not mention A'dityavarmá; but they expressly state that Chandráditya was the elder brother of Vikramáditya I. Whether Chandráditya himself actually reigned, is not clear. But Vijayamahádevi reigned after his death,—probably as regent during the childhood of a son, whose subsequent death lead to the accession of Vikramáditya I.

Amberá.

Of Amberá, we know nothing, except from the copper-plate grant from Hosur in Maisur, published by Mr. Rice, which may, or may not, be genuine.[6]

Vikramáditya I.

Of Vikramáditya I., also called Vikramáditya-Satyásraya, we have three genuine grants;—two are from the Karnul District, and are

---

1 *Ind. Ant.*, Vol. VI., p. 85; and Vol. X., p. 132. 2 *Id.*, Vol. VIII., p. 273.

3 The Miraj plates, and some subsequent inscriptions based on them, introduce two more generations into the genealogy, and make a certain Nadamari the son of Pulikesi II.,—A'dityavarmá the son of Nadamari,—and Vikramáditya I. the son of A'dityavarmá, and therefore the great-grandson, instead of the son, of Pulikesi II. But this is a pure mistake, based on imperfect tradition. *Ind. Ant.*, Vol. VI., p. 75, and Vol. X., p. 133.

4 *Ind. Ant.*, Vol. XI., p. 66. 5 *Id.*, Vol. VII., p. 163; and Vol. VIII., p. 44.

6 *Id.*, Vol. VIII., p. 89; and *Mysore Inscriptions*, p. 298.

dated in the third and tenth years of his reign, but without any reference to the Saka era;[1] the third is from Haidarábád in the Dekkan, and is not dated at all.[2] The exact commencement of his reign is, therefore, not known; but, as it terminated in Saka 602 (A.D. 680-1) or 603, and as he reigned for at least ten years, it cannot have been later than Saka 592 or 593. There is another grant from the Karnul District, which professes to be of the reign of Vikramáditya I.; but it is undated and very corrupt.[3] There is also another copper-plate grant, from Kurtakoti in the Dhárwád District, which professes to be dated in Saka 532 (A.D. 610-1), in the sixteenth year of his reign; but, for the reasons set forth in full in my notice of it, it is a forgery of the ninth or tenth century A.D.[4] The Karnul and Haidarábád grants, and the inscriptions of his successors, speak of Vikramáditya I. as riding forth to battle on his horse of the breed called Chitrakantha,[5] —seizing the city of Kánchi, after defeating the leader of the Pallavas who had been the cause of the humiliation and temporary destruction of his family,—defeating the kings of Chola and Pándya and Kerala, and the Kalabhras,—acquiring for himself the regal splendour of his father, which had been obscured by a confederacy of three kings,—and effecting the subordination of the whole kingdom to one sovereign in his own person. The second of his inscriptions mentions, apparently as his vassal, Devasakti, the king of the Sendrakas.

Vinayáditya.

Vikramáditya I. was succeeded, in Saka 602 (A.D. 680-1) or Saka 603, by his son Vinayáditya,—also called Vinayáditya-Satyásraya, Rájásraya or 'the asylum of kings,' and, if the Miraj plates may be trusted on this point, Yuddhamalla, or 'the wrestler or champion in war,'—who continued to reign up to about the middle of Saka 618 (A.D. 697-8). We have six inscriptions of his time,—a stone-tablet at Lakshmeswar within the limits of the Dhárwád District,[6] dated Saka 608 (A.D. 686-7), the seventh year of his reign, while his victorious camp was at the city of Raktapura;[7] a copper-plate grant from 'Togurshode,'[8] dated Saka 611 (A.D. 689-90), the tenth year of his reign, while his victorious camp was on the bank of the river Pampá, or the Tungabhadrá; a copper-plate grant from some unspecified place in the Karnul District or in Maisur,[9] dated Saka 613 (A.D. 691-2), the eleventh year of his reign, while his victorious camp was at the city of Elumpundale; a copper-plate grant from Sorab in Maisur,[10] dated Saka 614 (A.D. 692-3), the thirteenth year of his reign, while his victorious camp was at the village of Chitrasedu in the Toravara or

---

1 *Ind. Ant.*, Vol. X., p. 244.

2 *Id.*, Vol. VI., p. 75.

3 *Id.*, Vol. X., p. 244.

4 *Id.*, Vol. VII., p. 217.

5 'Speckle-throated.'

6 *Ind. Ant.*, Vol. VII., p. 112.

7 Raktapura would seem to have been a second ancient name of Puligere, Pulikaranagara, Purigere, or Lakshmeswar;—Lat. 15° 8′ N., Long. 75° 32′ E.

8 *Ind. Ant.*, Vol. VI., p. 85; *P. S. and O.-C. Inscriptions*, No. 14. I at first thought that this place was the 'Togarsagooda' of the maps, in the Shikárpur Táluká in Maisur. But I have since found a village, the name of which is given as 'Togurshode' in the map, and which is probably the place where this grant was really found, in the Karnul District,—in about Lat. 15° 28′ N., Long. 78° 29′ E.

9 *Id.*, Vol. VI., p. 88; *P. S. and O.-C. Inscriptions*, No. 15.

10 *P. S. and O.-C. Inscriptions*, No. 16; and see *Ind. Ant.*, Vol. VI., p. 94. —This grant is further dated on Saturday, at the time of the sun's commencing his progress to the north, under the constellation Rohini. This is the earliest instance yet known of the day of the week being mentioned in an inscription.

Toramara country; a copper-plate grant from Harihar in Maisur,[1] dated Saka 616 (A.D. 694-5), the fourteenth year of his reign, while his victorious camp was at the village of Karanjapatragráma in the neighbourhood of Hareshapura, which may perhaps be Harihar itself;[2] and an undated stone-tablet[3] at Balagámve in Maisur.[4] His warlike expeditions appear from the inscriptions to have been very numerous and extensive. He is described as arresting the extremely exalted power of the Pallava, the lord of Kánchi, whose kingdom consisted of three component dominions,—as causing the rulers of Kavera and Párasika and Simhala, or Ceylon, and other islands, to pay tribute to him,—as bringing the Pallavas, the Kalabhras, the Haihayas, the Vilas, the Malavas, the Cholas, and the Pándyas, into a similar state of servitude with the A'luvas and the Gangas, who were hereditarily subject to him,—and as acquiring the *pálidhvaja*[5] and other regal insignia, by crushing the lord of all the region of the north. A comparison of the fourth and fifth of his inscriptions noted above shews that his campaign against the Pallavas, the Kalabhras, &c., took place in Saka 615-6. The Balagámve tablet mentions, apparently as his vassal, Pogilli, the king of the Sendrakas. Vinayáditya seems to have fully restored the pristine power of his dynasty; and probably he made Vátápi again the capital.

Vijayáditya.

Vinayáditya was succeeded, in the month of A'shádha or of Srávana of Saka 618 (A.D. 696-7),[6] by his son Vijayáditya, also called Vijayáditya-Satyásraya, who continued to reign up to Saka 655 (A.D. 733-4). Of his time we have seven inscriptions,—one on a pillar in a temple called the Kallamatha at Bádámi,[7] dated Saka 621 (A.D. 699-700), the third year of his reign, while he was reigning at the capital of Vátápi; a copper-plate grant, from Nerur in the Sáwantwádi State,[8] dated Saka 622 (A.D. 700-1), the fourth year of his reign, while his victorious camp was at the city of Rásenanagara, which may perhaps be Rásin in the Ahmadnagar District;[9] another copper-plate grant from Nerur,[10] dated Saka 627 (A.D. 705-6), the tenth year of his reign; an inscription on the wall of the Huchchimalligudi temple at Aihole,[11] dated in the thirteenth year and the third month of his reign, and consequently in Saka 630 (A.D. 708-9); a stone-tablet at Lakshmeswar[12] dated Saka 651 (A.D. 729-30), the thirty-fourth year of his reign, while his victorious camp was at the city of Raktapura; an undated inscription on a pillar in the porch of the temple of Mahákutesvara near Bádámi;[13]

---

1 *Ind. Ant.*, Vol. VII., p. 300. 2 Lat. 14° 31′ N., Long. 75° 52′ E.

3 *P. S. and O.-C. Inscriptions*, No. 152; and see *Ind. Ant.*, Vol. VI., p. 94.—This is the earliest known stone-tablet that has any emblems, beyond a floral device, at the top of it; the emblem here is an elephant, standing, and is probably the emblem of the Sendraka family.

4 Lat. 14° 24′ N., Long. 75° 18′ E.

5 *Ind. Ant.*, Vol. VII., p. 111, note 25, and p. 245, note 6; and Vol. IX., p. 129, note 33.

6 *Id.*, Vol. VIII., p. 24. 7 *Id.*, Vol. X., p. 60. 8 *Id.*, Vol. IX., p. 125.

9 Lat. 18° 26′ N., Long. 47° 59′ E. It seems to be the Rásiyana which is mentioned in the Rádhanpur grant of the Ráshtrakuta king Govinda III. (*Ind. Ant.*, Vol. VI., p. 59).

10 *Ind. Ant.*, Vol. IX., p. 130. 11 *Id.*, Vol. VIII., p. 284.

12 *Id.*, Vol. VII., p. 112. 13 *Id.*, Vol. X., p. 102.

and a stone-tablet at Pattadakal,[1] the ancient Kisuvolal and Pattada-Kisuvolal, in the Kaládgi District.[2] He is spoken of in the inscriptions as a king who maintained the supremacy acquired by his father in the north and by his grandfather in the south; but, no campaigns undertaken by himself being mentioned, his reign seems to have been a peaceful one. It was in his time that the temple of the god Vijayesvara, now called the temple of Samgamesvara, at Pattadakal, was built.

Vikramáditya II.

Vijayáditya was succeeded, in Saka 655 (A.D. 733-4), by his eldest son Vikramáditya II., also called Vikramáditya-Satyásraya, who continued to reign up to Saka 669 (A.D. 747-8). Of his time we have one dated inscription,—a stone-tablet at Lakshmeswar,[3] dated Saka 656 (A.D. 734-5), the second year of his reign, while his victorious camp was at the city of Raktapura; and seven undated inscriptions,—a copper-plate grant from Nerur;[4] an inscription on the gateway of the Durga temple at Aihole;[5] two inscriptions on two pillars in the eastern gateway of the temple of the god Virupáksha, formerly Lokesvara, at Pattadakal;[6] two inscriptions on two pillars in the east porch of the same temple;[7] and an inscription on a pillar in the house of Parappa Pujári, close to the same temple.[8] The Pattadakal inscriptions tell us that his wife was Lokamahádevi, of the Haihaya family, and that the temple of Lokesvara was built for her, in commemoration of her husband having three times conquered the Pallavas of Kánchi. With this exception, his own inscriptions give no historical details. But the inscription of his son, Kirttivarmá II., to be noticed below, tells us that, determined to uproot the Pallavas, who had obscured the splendour of former kings of his lineage and who were the natural enemies of the Chalukyas, he made a sudden and expeditious incursion into the district of Tudáka, slew the Pallava king named Nandipotavarmá, who came to oppose him, and entered Kánchi, which, however, he refrained from destroying; also that he grievously distressed the Pándya, Chola, Kerala, Kalabhra, and other kings, and that he set up his pillar of victory on the shores of the southern ocean.

Kirttivarmá II.

Vikramáditya II. was succeeded, in Saka 669 (A.D. 747-8), by his son Kirttivarmá II., also called Kirttivarma-Satyásraya. The only inscription of his time that we have is the Wokkaleri grant, published by Mr. Rice,[9] dated Saka 679 (A.D. 757-8), the eleventh year of his reign, while his victorious camp was at the village of Bhandáragavittage, or perhaps Bhantáragavittage, on the northern bank of the river Bhimarathi. This fact, that his only known inscription comes from Maisur, the grant recorded in it being made at a village lying in the vicinity of Banawási and Hángal, —coupled with the statement of the Miraj plates that "through him the regal fortunes of the Chalukyas became impeded on the earth," and with what I shall have to say below regarding the

---

1 *Ind. Ant.* Vol. X., p. 165.
2 Lat. 15° 57′ N., Long. 75° 52′ E.
3 *Id.*, Vol. VII., p. 110.
4 *Id.*, Vol. IX., p. 132.
5 *Id.*, Vol. VII., p. 285.
6 *Id.*, Vol. X., pp. 162 to 165.
7 *Id.*, Vol. X., pp. 166 and 167.
8 *Id.*, Vol. X., p. 168.
9 *Id.*, Vol. VIII., p. 23.

Ráshtrakuta kings,—shows that, in the time of Kirttivarmá II., about the early part or the middle of the eighth century A.D., the Chalukyas were expelled from the Kanarese districts of the Bombay Presidency, which then came under the sway of the Ráshtrakutas.

Bhima I., Kirttivarmá III., Taila I., Vikramáditya III., Bhima II., Ayyana I., and Vikramáditya IV.

The termination of the reign of Kirttivarmá II. has not yet been fixed. So far as our information goes, he left no offspring, and the succession went back to his uncle, Bhima I., the younger son of Vijayáditya, or to his descendants. But we have no further authentic records belonging to the dynasty itself, till we come to the time of Taila II. We are dependent for the intermediate names entirely upon the Miraj plates, and the interval,—from Saka 679 (A.D. 757-8), the last recorded date for Kirttivarmá II., to Saka 895 (A.D. 973-4), the commencement of the reign of Taila II.,—being occupied only by seven generations, of which only five are subsequent in degree to Kirttivarmá II., it is pretty clear that the genealogy is not altogether reliable here, and that some steps must be wanting. About this I shall have more to say when I come to treat of the Western Chálukyas, as restored under Taila II. So far as the Miraj plates go, we have no record of Bhima I., Kirttivarmá III., Taila I., Vikramáditya III., and Bhima II., beyond the mere mention of their names; and of Ayyana I., all that we are told is that he repaired the fortunes of his race by marrying a daughter of Krishna, who was probably the Ráshtrakuta king Krishna II. or Akálavarsha I.,—and of Vikramáditya IV., that he married Bonthádevi or Vonthádevi, the daughter of Lakshmana, of the family of the kings of Chedi.[1] The Ráshtrakuta inscriptions, however, show that the power of the Chalukyas, though broken, was not annihilated, and that they made several, though unsuccessful, attempts to assert themselves. And it is probable that Taila I. and Ayyana I. are the Taila and Ayyapa of the Begur inscription,[2] which records that Ayyapa was killed in battle against a certain Viramahendra, who was perhaps, as Mr. Rice suggests, a Pallava king.[3] But, with these exceptions, we practically lose sight of the Western Chalukyas, and have as yet no clue as to what became of them, from the time of Kirttivarmá II. to the restoration of the dynasty by Taila III., about two centuries later.

---

1 *i.e.* of the Kalachuri dynasty of Tripura or Tewar,—General Cunningham, *Archæological Reports*, Vol. IX., p. 85.

2 *P. S. and O.-C. Inscriptions*, No. 247.

3 *Mysore Inscriptions*, p. lxiii.

SECTION V.

THE RA'SHTRAKUTAS.

So far we find that, from the first appearance of the Chalukyas in this part of the country, in the fifth century A.D., the Kanarese districts of the Bombay Presidency were held by them, with short periods of interruption of their power caused by the invasions of the Pallavas and other kings, down to about the early part or the middle of the eighth century A.D. Their sway over this part of the country then ceased entirely for a time. This was due to an invasion by the Ráshtrakuta kings, who, like their predecessors, came from the north. The chief exponent of the records of this dynasty has been Dr. Bühler.[1] The inscriptions of this dynasty edited by Bál Gangádhar Sástri, Mr. Wathen, Mr. Prinsep, and General Sir George LeGrand Jacob, require to be revised from the original plates and prepared for critical republication, and are being now so treated by myself; and I have also a few more inscriptions which have not yet been published at all. But, as I have not many materials additional to those accessible to Dr. Bühler, I can do little more than follow in his track,—at any rate as far as the time of Amoghavarsha I.

It is difficult to say when there was first a Ráshtrakuta kingdom. The earliest notices that we have of the family are contained in the Western Chalukya inscriptions. Thus, the Miraj plates tell us that Jayasimha I. restored the fortunes of the Chalukya dynasty by defeating, amongst others, one Indra of the Ráshtrakuta family, who was the son of Krishna,[2] and who possessed an army of eight hundred elephants; and there is little doubt that A'ppáyika-Govinda, who, as we are told in the Aihole Meguti inscription, came from the north and invaded the Chalukya kingdom with his troops of elephants and was repulsed by Pulikesi II., also belonged to this same dynasty. It is plain, therefore, that in the fifth and sixth centuries A.D. the Ráshtrakuta dynasty was one of considerable importance in central or in northern India. The later inscriptions state that the Ráshtrakutas were of the Somavamsa or lunar race, and were descendants of Yadu. Dr. Burnell seems inclined to look upon the family as of Drávidian origin, as he gives 'Ráshtra' as

---

1 His chief paper on the dynasty is in the *Ind. Ant.*, Vol. VI., pp. 59 &c.

2 Some silver coins, found at Devaláná in the Báglán Táluká of the Násik District, and on palæographical grounds attributed by Dr. Bhau Dáji to the end of the fourth century A.D. (*Jour. Bo. Br. R. As. Soc.*, Vol. XII., p. 213), clearly have on them the name of Krishnarája, as is shown by General Cunningham, who attributes them to this early Ráshtrakuta king Krishna, who was the father of the Indra defeated by Jayasimha I., and whose date accordingly must be about A.D. 375 to 400 (*Archæological Reports*, Vol. IX., p. 29).

an instance of the Sanskritsing of Drávidian names, and considers it to be a mythological perversion for 'Ratta,' which is the same as the Kanarese and Telugu 'Reddi.'[1] Dr. Bühler is unable to record any opinion, as to "whether the Ráshtrakutas were an A'ryan Kshatriya, *i. e.* Rájput, race, which immigrated into the Dekkan from the north like the Chalukyas, or a Drávidian family which was received into the A'ryan community after the conquest of the Dekkan." The earliest inscriptions, at any rate, show them as coming from the north. And, whatever may be their origin,—as the word *ráshtrakuta* is used in many inscriptions of other dynasties as the equivalent of *ráshtrapati*, *i.e.* as an official word meaning 'the head-man or governor of a country or district,' it appears to me that the selection of it as a dynastic name implies that, prior to attaining independent sovereignty, the Ráshtrakutas were feudal chiefs under some previous dynasty of which they have not preserved any record.

The accompanying table gives the genealogy of the dynasty, as far as it is known at present. In the last three generations it does not altogether agree with the genealogy given in the Khárepátan plates.[2] But those plates contain a grant, dated Saka 930 (A.D. 1008-9), the Kilaka *samvatsara*, of Ráhurája, belonging to a branch of the Siláhára family in the Konkan, a feudatory of the Western Chálukya king Satyásraya II.; and the Ráshtrakuta genealogy, as given in that inscription, is not of necessity to be accepted as correct in all its details.

Dantivarmá I., and Indra I.

The first two names are taken from an inscription of Dantidurga or Dantivarmá II. in the Elurá caves.[3] But it furnishes no historical information in respect of them; and none of the other inscriptions carry the genealogy back beyond Govinda I.

Govinda I., and Karka I. or Kakka I.

Regarding these two, again, we have no information beyond the mention of their names. No historical facts are recorded in respect of them.

Indra II.

In connection with Indra II., all that we are told is that his wife, whose name is not given, was the daughter of a Chalukya father and a Somavamsa mother. It is a justifiable inference from this fact, that the Ráshtrakutas had not yet come into any hostile contact with the Western Chalukyas, or made any attempt to dispossess them.

Dantidurga or Dantivarmá II.

Dantidurga, or Dantivarmá II., also called Khadgávaloka, is the first of whom we have any historical details. We have two inscriptions of his time,—the inscription in the Elurá caves, of which I have spoken above, and the plates from Sámangad[4] in the Kolhápur territory, dated Saka 675 (A.D. 753-4).[5] In the latter we are told that his victorious elephants ploughed up the banks of the river Revá, or the Narmadá,—that he acquired supreme dominion by conquering Vallabha,—and that he easily defeated the army of

---

1 *South-Indian Palæography*, p. X. 2 *Jour. Bo. Br. R. As. Soc.*, Vol. I., p. 209.
3 No. 10, p. 92, of the separate pamphlets of the Archæological Survey of Western India. 4 Lat. 16° 11' N., Long. 74° 29' E.
5 *Ind. Ant.*, Vol. XI., p. 108.—This is the earliest known inscription in which the date is expressed by figures arranged according to the decimal system of notation.

ENEALOGI OF THE RASHTRAKUTA DYNASTY.

- Dantivarmá I.
  - Indra I.
    - Govinda I.
      - Karka I., or Kakka I.
        - Indra II.
          - Dantidurga, or Dantivarmá II. (Saka 675.)
        - Krishna I.
          - Govinda II.
          - Dhruva, Dhora, Nirupama I., or Dhárávarsha.
            - Govinda III., Prabhutavarsha I., Jagattunga I., Jagadrudra I., or Vallabhanarendra I. (Saka 725 and 729.)
              - Amoghavarsha I. (Saka 778 and 799.)
                - Krishna II., or Akálavarsha I. (Saka 797 and 833.)
                  - Jagattunga II., or Jagadrudra II.
                    - *By his wife Lakshmi.*
                      - Indra IV., or Nityavarsha.
                        - *(Not named.)*
                        - Govinda V., Suvarnavarsha II., or Vallabhanarendra II. (Saka 855.)
                    - *By his wife Govindámbá.*
                      - Krishna III.
                      - Amoghavarsha II.
                        - Khottiga.
                        - Krishna IV., Nirupama II., or Akálavarsha II. (Saka 867 and 878.)
                          - Kakka III., (Karka III.), Kakkala, Karkara, Amoghavarsha III., or Vallabhanarendra III. (Saka 894.)
                            - Jákabbe, or Jákaladevi, *(married to the Western Chálukya king*
            - Indra III.
              - Karka II., (Kakka II.), or Suvarnavarsha I. (Saka 734.)
              - Govinda IV., or Prabhutavarsha II. (Saka 749.)

the Karnátaka, which was expert in dispersing the kings of Kánchi and Kerala, the Cholas, the Pándyas, Sri-Harsha, and Vajrata. Taking these statements, and comparing the date of Dantidurga with the date of the Western Chalukya king Kirttivarmá II., the only ruler of the Karnátaka with whom he can have come in contact; and bearing in mind that the only known grant of Kirttivarmá II. comes from Maisur,—we have it clearly established that it was Dantidurga who dispossessed the Western Chalukyas of their kingdom in the Kanarese districts of the Bombay Presidency, and established the Ráshtrakutas in their place. It must have been by his victory over the Western Chalukyas that he acquired the title of *Prithivivallabha*, or 'favourite of the world,' which had always been borne by the kings of that dynasty. And 'Vallabha', too, was in more instances than one a Chalukya name or title.

Krishna I.

Dantidurga was succeeded by his uncle Krishna I., also called Vallabha I. There are two explanations given of this. The Kardá plates state that Dantidurga died childless. While the Baroda plates state that Dantidurga fell into evil ways, and that consequently Krishna I. ousted him and appropriated the sovereignty for the good of his race. He continued the conquests of Dantidurga, and is described as dispersing the darkness which was the race of the Chalukyas, and as depriving them of the goddess of sovereignty. An allusion to the same fact is also made in the statement that he changed into a deer, *i.e.* that he put to flight, the *Mahávaráha*, or 'the great boar,'—the family-emblem of the Chalukyas. It is also said that he established himself at the hill, or hill-fort, of Elápura, where there was a famous temple of the god Svayambhu-Siva. This place has not been identified, I believe; but it seems to me not unlikely that it is Yellápur[1] in North Kanara, in the Western Ghauts.

Govinda II.

Krishna I. left two sons. Of the elder, Govinda II., also called Vallabha II., we have no historical details, except that he was dethroned by his younger brother.

Dhruva.

The younger son then succeeded,—Dhruva, or Nirupama I., also called Dhora, Iddhatejas, Dhárávarsha, and Kalivallabha. Of these, the name Dhora is simply the Prákrit correlative of the Sanskrit form Dhruva. We have an undated Old-Kanarese inscription of this king, on a pillar in the north porch of the temple of the god Lokesvara or Virupáksha at Pattadakal in the Kaládgi District,[2] in which he is called Dhárávarsha-Kaliballaha,—Kaliballaha being the Prákrit correlative of the Sanskrit form Kalivallabha. Among the exploits of Dhruva, it is recorded that he conquered and imprisoned the Ganga king, and that he humbled the pride of the Pallavas.

Govinda III.

Dhruva was succeeded by his eldest son Govinda III. or Prabhutavarsha I., also called Jagattunga I., Jagadrudra I., Vallabhanarendra I., Srivallabha, and Prithvivallabha. Of his time there are four inscriptions,—a copper-plate grant in Sir Walter Elliot's possession, dated Saka 726 for 725 (A.D. 803-4), the Subhánu or Svabhánu *sam*-

---

1 Lat. 14° 59′ N., Long. 74° 47′ E.; the chief town of the Táluká of the same name.

2 *Third Archæological Report*, p. 123; *P. S. and O.-C. Inscriptions*, No. 60.

vatsara;[1] the Wani-Dindori plates from the Násik District, dated Saka 730 for 728 (A.D. 806-7), the Vyaya *samvatsara*;[2] the Rádhanpur plates from Gujarát, dated Saka 730 for 729 (A.D. 807-8), the Sarvajit *samvatsara*;[3] and an undated fragment at Lakshmeswar in the Dhárwád District, in which he is called Sriballaha, *i. e.* Srivallabha. The early part of his reign was occupied with wars and victories in Gujarát and Central India, with which we are not concerned in this paper. The first of the grants that I have mentioned above gives us Gámundabbe as the name of his queen, and records a grant that was made by him when, having conquered Dantiga, the ruler of Kánchi, he came to the banks of the Tungabhadrá on his way to demand tribute, and there had some sport with wild boars at a sacred place called Rámesvara,[4] and was consequently pleased with the place. This expedition to the Tungabhadrá, and this conquest of the Pallavas, are mentioned in his other inscriptions, which tell us also that the ruler of Vengi, *i.e.* his contemporary of the Eastern Chalukya family,[5] was one of his vassals, and was employed to build for him the high walls of a town or fortress. His dominions, therefore, extended from the western to the eastern coast, and from the Vindhya mountains and Márwád in the north to at least the Tungabhadrá in the south. His second and third grants were issued from Mayurakhandi or Mayurakhindi, which Dr. Bühler[6] has identified with Morkhanda, a hill-fort north of Wani in the Násik District.[7]

Indra III., Karka II., and Govinda IV.

In the time of Govinda III. there seems to have been a partial division of the Ráshtrakuta kingdom; and his younger brother, Indra III., received from him the newly conquered province of Láta or Central and southern Gujarát. This established the separate Ráshtrakuta kingdom of Gujarát. Indra III. was succeeded in this kingdom, first by his eldest son Karka II., also called Suvarnavarsha I. and Látesvara, of whose time we have the Baroda plates, dated Saka 734 (A.D. 812-3), and issued from Siddhasami;[8] and then by his second son,[9] Govinda IV., also called Prabhuta-

---

1 I have no precise information as to where these plates were found; but it was somewhere in the Kanarese country, and the inscription is in the Old-Kanarese language.—This is the earliest known instance of the use in inscriptions of the cycle of sixty *samvatsaras*. We find it, therefore, first introduced into the Kanarese country by the Ráshtrakutas. But,—as it is not used in the subsequent grants of Karka II. and Govinda IV., who constitute what Dr. Bühler has named the Gujarát branch of the family; whereas it is used in all the subsequent southern grants of the family,—it is plain that the Ráshtrakutas did not import the cycle from the north, but found it already in use in the south, though not among the Chalukyas.—The Saka years and the *samvatsaras*, as recorded in inscriptions, do not always agree correctly. In the present instance, by the *Tables* in Brown's *Carnatic Chronology*, the Svabhánu *samvatsara* was Saka 725, and Saka 726 was the Tárana *samvatsara*. The error is, I believe, always in the Saka date, and not in the name of the *samvatsara*.

2 *Jour. R. As. Soc.*, O. S., Vol. V., p. 343.

3 *Ind. Ant.*, Vol. VI., p. 59.

4 An island a few miles north of the junction of the Tungá and the Bhadrá; *Mysore Inscriptions*, p. lvii. Mr. Rice places it, in his map of ancient Maisur, in the position occupied in modern maps by 'Anavaree,'—Lat. 14° 4′ N., Long. 75° 49′ E.

5 Apparently Vijayáditya, also called Narendramrigarája, who reigned from about Saka 710 to about Saka 750.

6 *Ind. Ant.*, Vol. VI., p. 64.

7 Lat. 20° 24′ N., Long. 74° E.

8 *Jour. Beng. As. Soc.*, Vol. VIII., p. 292.

9 The genealogies given by Dr. Bühler in *Ind. Ant.*, Vol. V., p. 145, and Vol. VI., p. 72, make Govinda IV. the son, and not the younger brother, of Karka II., and consequently the grandson, and not the son, of Indra III. This must be only a clerical error, or a printer's mistake.

varsha II., of whose time we have the Kávi plates, dated Saka 749 (A.D. 827-8), and issued from Bharukachchha or Broach.[1] We are not concerned any further in this paper with the history of these three kings, whose line, indeed, seems to have died out with Govinda IV. Dr. Bühler considers that they were only vassals of their relatives of the main line.

Amoghavarsha I.

In the main line, Govinda III. was succeeded by his son, Amoghavarsha I. This is only a title; his real name is unknown. The only historical facts recorded of him are that he defeated the Chalukyas, and was pacified by them at a place named Vingavalli, which is evidently a Kanarese name, but which I cannot identify,—and that he either founded, or located himself at, the city of Mányakheta, which became the capital of his descendants. This city has been satisfactorily identified by Dr. Bühler with Málkhed[2] in the Nizám's Dominions, about ninety miles in a south-easterly direction from Sholápur. We have six inscriptions of his time,—two in the Kanheri caves, which are dated Saka 775 for 773 (A.D. 851-2), the Prajápati *samvatsara,* and Saka 799 (A.D. 877-8), and record that, during the reign of Kapardi II. of the Konkana branch of the Siláhára family, the whole of the Konkana was presented by Amoghavarsha I., apparently to Kapardi II.;[3] one at Mantrawádi, near Bankápur in the Dhárwád District, dated Saka 787 (A.D. 865-6), the Párthiva *samvatsara*; one, undated, at Nidagundi in the same neighbourhood, which records that his feudatory, Bankeyarasa, of the Chellaketana family, had the government of the Banavási Twelve-thousand, the Belgali Three-hundred, the Kundarage Seventy, the Kundur Five-hundred, and the Purigere, *i.e.* the Puligere or Lakshmeswar, Three-hundred; one, undated, at Kyásanur near Hángal, which records that his feudatory, Samkaraganda, of the same family, had the government of the Banavási province; and one at Soratur, near Gadag in the Dhárwád District, dated in the Virodhi *samvatsara, i. e.* Saka 791 (A.D. 869-70), which records that his feudatory A'haváditya, belonging to a family which apparently was called the A'davavamsa, was then governing the Kuppeya-Purigere province.

Krishna II., or Akálavarsha I.

He was succeeded by his son, Krishna II., or Akálavarsha I., of whose time we have six inscriptions,—one, undated, at Kyásanur, in which he is called Kandaravallabha, and which records that his feudatory, the *Mahásámantádhipati* Samkaraganda, who must be the Samkaraganda of the Chellaketana family mentioned above as the feudatory of his father Amoghavarsha I., was governing the Banavási province; one, the date of which is unfortunately quite illegible in the photograph,[4] at Tálgund in Maisur,[5] in which he is called Khandaraballaha, and which mentions again the same Samkaraganda as his feudatory in charge of the Banavási province; one at Nandwádige[6] in the Kaládgi District, dated Saka 822 for 824

1 *Ind. Ant.*, Vol. V., p. 144.
2 The 'Mulkaid' of the maps; Lat. 17° 12' N., Long. 77° 14' E.
3 Pandit Bhagwánlál Indraji; *Jour. Bo. Br. R. As. Soc.*, Vol. XIII., p. 11.
4 *P. S. and O.-C. Inscriptions*, No. 213.
5 The 'Taulagoonda' of the maps; Lat. 14° 25' N., Long. 75° 19' E.
6 The 'Nundarudagi' of the maps, fourteen miles to the east from Hungund.

(A.D. 902-3), the Dundubhi *samvatsara*, in which he is called Akálavarsha;[1] one at Mulgund[2] in the Dhárwád District, dated Saka 824, the Dundubhi *samvatsara*, in which he is called Krishnavallabha;[3] one at A'dur near Hángal, dated Saka 826 (A.D. 904-5), the Raktákshi *samvatsara*, in which he is called Akálavarsha, and which mentions some other *Mahásámanta* of the Chellaketana family, whose name is very doubtful, as having the government of the Banavási Twelve-thousand; and one at Aihole in the Kaládgi District, dated Saka 831 for 833 (A.D. 911-2), the Prajápati *samvatsara*, in which he is called Kannara.[4] In two of the later inscriptions of the Rattas of Saundatti and Belgaum, he is called Krishna-Kandhara and Krishna-Kandhára.[5] And in one of these two passages he has the title of *Kandhára-puravar-ádhisvara*, or 'supreme lord of Kandhárapura, the best of cities:' there may have been an original city of the Ráshtrakutas, named Kandhárapura; but the present mention of it is as yet an isolated one. He is also mentioned in the earliest of the Ratta inscriptions, as reigning in Saka 797 (A.D. 875-6), the Manmatha *samvatsara*;[6] but he must at that time have been only the *Yuvarája*, or heir-apparent and viceroy, for the southern part of his father's dominions. It is plain, therefore, that at the end of the ninth century A.D. he held all the Kanarese districts of this Presidency above the Ghauts. The two later Ratta inscriptions mentioned above also assert that he was the progenitor of their family. But this can hardly be the case; though it was he who first raised them, in the person of Prithviráma, to the rank and authority of *Mahásámantas* or *Mahámandalesvaras*. Nothing more is known of him, except that his wife was the younger sister of Sankuka, and the daughter of Kokkala or Kokkalla, king of Chedi, who is said in the Kardá plates to be of the Haihaya family, and in the Sángli plates to be of the lineage of Sahasrárjuna, *i.e.* Kártavirya, or Sahasrabáhu-Arjuna, prince of the Haihayas. This Kokkala or Kokkalla, king of Chedi, was, therefore, the first of that name in General Cunningham's genealogy of the Kalachuri kings of Tripura or Tewar.[7]

Jagattunga II., or Jagadrudra II.

Krishna II. was succeeded by his son, Jagattunga II., or Jagadrudra II. He had two wives. The Sángli plates tell us that he married Lakshmi, the daughter of Ranavigraha, who was the son of Kokkala, and had by her Indra IV., his immediate successor. The Kardá plates give the same name, Lakshmi, but state that she was the daughter of Samkaragana, lord of Chedi, and give also the same name, Indra, as that of his eldest son. But they also add that he set out on an expedition with the object of

---

1 *P. S. and O.-C. Inscriptions*, No. 85.—Through some mistake, which I do not now understand, I have spoken of it there and also in the *Ind. Ant.*, Vol. VII., p. 210, as being dated Saka 722, and of the time of Dhruva or of Govinda III.

2 Twelve miles to the south-west from Gadag.

3 *Jour. Bo. Br. R. As. Soc.*, Vol. IX., p. 190.

4 *P. S. and O.-C. Inscriptions*, No. 79.

5 Kannara, Kanhara, Kanhára, Kandhara, and Kandhára, all occur as the names of kings whose name in its Sanskrit form is Krishna. In the first and second of his inscriptions, Kandara and Khandara must be intended for Kandhara.

6 *Jour. Bo. Br. R. As. Soc.*, Vol. X., p. 194.

7 *Archæological Reports*, Vol. IX., p. 85. Sankuka, however, is not mentioned in that genealogy.

making the whole world subordinate to one sovereign in himself, and then, in Chedi, married Govindámbá, the daughter of his maternal uncle Samkaragana, and had by her two other sons, Krishna III. and Amoghavarsha II. These accounts as to the pedigree of his wives can be properly reconciled only by taking Samkaragana and Ranavigraha to be one and the same person, and to be a brother of the daughter of Kokkalla whom Krishna II. married; in this way Sankaragana would be the maternal uncle, as well as the father-in-law, of Jagattunga II. However this may be, this explicit statement of the double marriage of Jagattunga II. entirely removes some doubts that have been entertained as to the line of the succession, and the correctness of the genealogy, after him.[1]

Indra IV.

Jagattunga II. was succeeded immediately by his eldest son, Indra IV. or Nityavarsha. Of him all that we are told is that he married Dvijámbá, the daughter of Ammana, the son of Arjuna, who was the son of Kokkalla of the Haihaya family, *i.e.* Kokkalla I. of the Kalachuri dynasty, whom we have already mentioned.

Govinda V.

Indra IV. appears to have left two sons, the elder of whom, not named in the inscription, was quietly set aside by the younger, Govinda V., also called Suvarnavarsha II. and Vallabhanarendra II. We have one inscription of his time, the Sángli[2] plates, dated Saka 855 (A.D. 933-4), the Vijaya *samvatsara.*[3] His capital was Mányakheta; but we have no further details regarding him.

Krishna III., Amoghavarsha II., and Khottiga.

The succession then went to the second family of Jagattunga II. by his second wife Govindámbá, probably through Govinda V. dying without issue. There is at any rate nothing in the inscriptions to indicate that any act of forcible usurpation took place. It is not probable that Krishna III., and Amoghavarsha II., whose wife was Kundakadevi,[4] and Khottiga, actually reigned. The shortness of the interval between the date of the grant of Govinda V. and the date of the grant of Krishna IV., is against any such supposition.

Krishna IV.

Of Krishna IV., or Kannara, also called Nirupama II. and Akálavarsha II., we have five inscriptions,—two at Kyásanur in the Dhárwád District, dated Saka 868 for 867 (A.D. 945-6), the Visvávasu *samvatsara,*[5] in which he is called Kannara, and which record that his feudatory, the *Mahásámanta* Kali-Vitta, of the Chellaketana family, had the government of the Banavási province; one at Sálotgi[6] in the Kaládgi District, dated Saka 867 for 869 (A.D. 947-8), the Plavamga *samvatsara;*[7] one at Soratur[8] in the Dhárwád District, dated Saka 873 (A.D. 951-2), the Virodhikrit *samvatsara;*[9] and one at A'lur, near Hángal, dated Saka 877 for 878 (A.D. 956-7), the Nala *samvatsara,* in which again he is

---

[1] *Ind. Ant.*, Vol. I., p. 207; and Vol. VI., p. 65.
[2] Lat. 16° 52′ N., Long. 74° 38′ E.
[3] *Jour. Bo. Br. R. As. Soc.*, Vol. IV., p. 97.
[4] General Cunningham considers that she was the daughter of the Kalachuri king Yuvarája I. (*Archæol. Reports*, Vol. IX., p. 104). In the same *Report*, p. 80, he makes her the daughter of Lakshmana, the son of Yuvarája I.; but this must be an oversight. It is likely enough that she was of the Kalachuri family, and was the daughter of Yuvarája I.; but the Ráshtrakuta inscription which mentions her tells us nothing of her father except that his name was Yuvarájadeva.
[5] One of them is given in the Elliot *MS. Collection*, Vol. II., p. 673.
[6] Six miles to the south-east from Indi.
[7] *Ind. Ant.*, Vol. I., p. 205.
[8] Twelve miles to the south from Gadag.
[9] Elliot *MS. Collection*, Vol. II., p. 673.

called Kannara. The third of these records that Krishna IV. was then reigning at Mányakheta. Mr. K. T. Telang, who published this inscription, translated the words *pravardhamána-parama-kalyána-vijayodyama*, in line 4, by "engaged in reducing the prosperous and great Kalyána" (of the Western Chálukyas). This rendering, however, cannot be upheld; in the first place, if the city of Kalyána had been intended, the word *pura* would certainly have been used; and in the second place, it was not long, if at all, before Saka 975 (A.D. 1053-6), that Kalyána became a capital of the Western Chálukyas, in the reign of Somesvara I. The words, as they stand, are simply an expression of the continually increasing prosperity and victorious enterprise of Krishna IV.

Kakka III.

He was succeeded by his son, Kakka III., or Karka III.,—also called Kakkala, Karkara,[1] Amoghavarsha III., and Vallabhanarendra III., —the last of the dynasty of whom we have any record. There is one inscription of his time, the Kardá plates, dated Saka 894 (A.D. 972-3), the A'ngirasa *samvatsara*, while he was reigning at Mányakheta.[2] He is spoken of as conquering the Gurjara, the Huna, the Chola, and the Pándya kings; but no details are given. In Saka 895 (A.D. 973-4), the Srimukha *samvatsara*, he succumbed to, and probably was slain by, Taila II. of the Chálukya family; and the Ráshtrakuta dynasty then ceased to exist. The only offspring of Kakka III. of whom we have any mention is his daughter, Jákabbe or Jákaladevi, who became the wife of Taila II.

---

1 *Ind. Ant.*, Vol. VIII., p. 16. And the name is given probably in the same form, though the copy reads Kamkara, in an inscription at Mannugulli in the Kaládgi District (Elliot *MS. Collection*, Vol. I., p. 746).

2 *Jour. R. As. Soc.*, O. S., Vol. II., p. 379; and Vol. III., p. 49.

SECTION VI.

THE WESTERN CHA'LUKYAS.

Various allusions in the Ráshtrakuta inscriptions show that, all through the period of this obscuration of their power, the Chalukyas had repeatedly made attempts to re-assert themselves, but without success. These allusions, however, have no individuality about them. And,—with the exception of the possible notice of Taila I. and Ayyana I. in the Begur inscription,—practically we lose sight completely of the Chalukyas from the time of Kirttivarmá II. until the restoration of the dynasty by Taila II.[1] Of this restoration,

---

1 In the *Jour. R. As. Soc.*, N. S., Vol. XIV., p. 19, Mr. Rice has published an account of the Kanarese poet Pampa or Hampa, the great-grandson of Mánava-Somayáji of the city of Vengi, and states of him that "From his first work, the *A'di-Purána*, we learn that he was born in Saka 824 (A.D. 902-3). But his second work, the *Vikramárjunavijaya* or *Pampa-Bhárata*, which established his fame, tells us that both were written in the same year, Saka 863 (A.D. 941-2), and adds many particulars full of interest in regard to himself and the circumstances under which he wrote." Pampa claims as his patron a certain king Arikesari, whom he made the hero of his second poem, and to whom he allots the following descent;—1, Yuddhamalla, of the Chalukya family, who ruled over the *Sapádalaksha* or Lac-and-a-quarter country;—2, Arikesari, son of 1, who, with the ministers of the 'Bange rishaya' (? Vengi *vishaya*), penetrated into the kingdom of Nirupamadeva;—3, Narasimhabhadradeva, son of 2;—4, Dugdhamalla, son of 3;—5, Baddiga, eldest son of 4, who acquired the title of *Solada-Ganda*, and who, "as if seizing a crocodile, entered into the water and proudly seized Bhima";—6, Yuddhamalla, son of 5;—7, Narasimha, son of 6, who gave a territory to Erapa, subdued the chiefs of the seven Málala (?), plucked the goddess of victory from the arms of the Ghurjara *(sic)* king, and bathed his horse at the junction of the Ganges;—and finally, 8, Arikesari, son of 7 and his wife Chandránane, who protected Vijayáditya against the universal emperor Gujjiga or Gojjiga who attacked him.—As Mr. Rice points out, the only one of the Western Chalukya kings who bore the title of Yuddhamalla was Vinayáditya, who reigned from Saka 602 or 603 to 618. It should, however, be noted that, whether even he really had that title, depends upon the authenticity of the Miraj plates for that early period; and in respect of the succession for two generations after Pulikesi II. they are altogether wrong and unauthentic. Also, as he points out, there was a Ráshtrakuta king named Nirupama; in fact, two of them had that title,—Dhruva, and Krishna IV. But the earliest of them was Dhruva, and his date was about Saka 700, and at any rate cannot possibly have been earlier than Saka 675; and this seems too late for a son of Vinayáditya to have been his contemporary. As regards the other names,—Mr. Rice suggests that "Bhima may be the Chálukya who is denounced in such strong terms in the Rudradeva inscription." This suggestion is based on Mr. Rice's assumption (*Mysore Inscriptions*, p. xliv) that the inscription belongs unmistakeably to the middle of the ninth century A.D. But the real date of it (*Ind. Ant.*, Vol. XI., p. 9) is Saka 1084 (A.D. 1162-3). There is nothing in it to indicate that Bhima was of the Chálukya lineage. And, as he usurped the Western Chálukya dominions after the death of Taila III. in Saka 1084, it is plain that he cannot have been a contemporary of Pampa's king Baddiga, whose date would be about Saka 750. In respect of this name of Baddiga, Mr. Rice remarks that it "seems to have been a popular name at about this period; it occurs as that of the ruler of Kánchi in Saka 726, and as that of a Ratta" (*i.e.* Ráshtrakuta) "king." On the first point, however, he is wrong; as the real name in the inscription in question is Dantiga (see under the account of Govinda III.). And the Khárepátan plates, which alone mention the Ráshtrakuta king Baddiga, place him only three

there are many distinct records. The Khárepátan plates, for instance, after giving the Ráshtrakuta genealogy from Dantidurga down to Kakka III., or Kakkala as he is there called, state that he was defeated in war by the Chálukya king Tailapa. The Miraj plates, in the account of Taila II., tell us that by him "were easily cut asunder, in the field of battle, the two pillars of (*victory in*) war of Karkara, which belonged to the kingdom of the Ráshtrakuta family," and that by him "were lifted up the royal fortunes of the kingly favourites of the Chálukya family, which had been made to sink down by the deceitful practices of the Ráshtrakutas." A somewhat similar description is given in an inscription at Mannugulli in the Kaládgi District,[1] in which the name of the Ráshtrakuta king conquered by him is given as Kamkara in the copy, but is probably correctly given as Karkara in the original. And an inscription at Gadag in the Dhárwád District,[2] and another, based on the same model, at Kálige in the Nizám's Dominions,[3] tell us that Taila uprooted the Rattas, and slew Munja,[4] and killed the leader of the Pánchálas in war, and then reigned over the whole earth for twenty-

---

generations before Saka 930. The names of Erapa, the Ghurjara king, and Gojjiga, may be passed over; nothing very definite can be established by means of them either way. And finally, as regards Vijayáditya, who was protected against Gujjiga or Gojjiga by the second Arikesari,—this was *not* the name of the predecessor of Taila II., who restored the Western Chálukya dynasty in Saka 895. His predecessor was his father, Vikramáditya IV.; and, with the doubtful exception of a person named Vishnuvardhana-Vijayáditya, whose date was Saka 988 and who is said in the only inscription that mentions him to have been a son of Somesvara I., the name does not occur at all among the Western Chalukyas or Chálukyas after the king, the son of Vinayáditya, who reigned from Saka 618 to 655. It is worth noting, however, that this name did occur several times among the Eastern Chalukya kings of Vengi, to which city or country the poet Pampa belonged by birth;—*e.g.* in the case of the grandfather and the senior cousin of Amma II., and, apparently, also as a second name of Amma II. himself, who succeeded to the throne in Saka 867. So also, it may be noted, did the name of Yuddhamalla occur among the Eastern Chalukyas, in the second and fourth generations before Amma II. And, with respect to Pampa's statement that Yuddhamalla's kingdom was a Lac-and-a-quarter country,—from which Mr. Rice appears to draw some conclusion or other in support of the view that this Yuddhamalla was Vinayáditya, inasmuch as he specially states in a footnote that "the dominion of the Western Chálukyas is described in inscriptions as a 7½ *lakh* country,"—it is worth noting that this expression, a Seven-and-a-half-lac country, *is* applied to the kingdom, not of the Western Chálukyas, but of the Early Chalukyas, and not in any early and authentic passage, but only in the *farrago* of vague tradition and *Puránik* myths which was introduced into the preamble of the grants, of the eleventh century A.D., of Rájarája II. and others of the Chola successors of the Eastern Chalukya kings (see *Ind. Ant.*, Vol. VII., p. 244).—The poet Pampa further tells us that he wrote in the pithy or pure Kanarese of Puligere, the royal city; and that Arikesari rewarded him with a grant of the village of Dharmattiram in the Bachche Thousand. The Bachche Thousand is not otherwise known to me. But Puligere was the ancient name of Lakshmeswar, which is in the heart of the Kanarese country; and the neighbouring town of Dambal is called in inscriptions Dharmápura and Dharmavolal. We may, therefore, take it, as Mr. Rice does, that the Puligere of Pampa is the modern Lakshmeswar.—It will be interesting if we hereafter obtain any evidence of the existence of Western or Eastern Chalukyas at Lakshmeswar during the period of the Ráshtrakuta supremacy. Pampa's statements point rather to the Eastern than to the Western Branch. But none of the names given by him are mentioned in any of the thirty-three inscriptions known to me to be extant at Lakshmeswar, and ranging from early in the eighth to the sixteenth century A.D., or in the inscriptions at Dambal. And his statements are not *primâ-facie* sufficiently reliable to prove the fact of themselves on behalf of either Branch of the family, and much less to justify the introduction of a new set of names into the genealogy and history of the Western Branch.

1 Elliot *MS. Collection*, Vol. I., p. 746. 2 *Id.*, Vol. I., p. 370.
3 *Id.*, Vol. I., p. 415. 4 King of Málava; *Ind. Ant.*, Vol. V., p. 317.

four years, beginning with the Srimukha *samvatsara*. This fixes the restoration of the dynasty, and the commencement of his reign, in Saka 895 (A.D. 973-4), which was the Srimukha *samvatsara*. These Rattas, uprooted by Taila, were the Ráshtrakutas of Mányakheta,—not the Rattas of Saundatti and Belgaum, of whom an account will be given further on.

As I have intimated above, a comparison of the date of Saka 679 (A.D. 757-8) as the last recorded date of Kirttivarmá II., with that of Saka 895 (A.D. 973-4) as the commencement of the reign of Taila II., shows,—the interval of two hundred and sixteen years being occupied by only seven names, and practically by only five generations, as only five of those names are subsequent in degree to Kirttivarmá II.,—that the genealogy cannot be reliable here, and that some steps must be wanting in it. And,—whereas the Early and Western Chalukyas invariably call themselves Chalkyas, Chalikyas, or Chalukyas, (with the vowel of the first syllable short),—Taila II. and his descendants, except where the word occurs in verse and the metre necessitates the use of the older form Chalukya, always call themselves Chálukyas (with the vowel of the first syllable long), or 'descendants of a Chalukya.' These facts, taken together, suggest as an inevitable inference that Taila II. was not a direct lineal descendant of the youngest son of Vijayáditya, but came from some side-branch of the Chalukya stock. Where the break in the genealogy is to be fixed is not quite certain. The Gadag, Kálige, and Mannugulli inscriptions agree with the Miraj plates in making Taila II. the son of Vikramáditya IV. and Bonthádevi; but none of the inscriptions, except the Miraj plates and the stone-tablets based on them, give the name of the grandfather of Taila II. We may probably, therefore, accept as correct the statement that his father was Vikramáditya IV., and place the break in the genealogy between Ayyana I. and Vikramáditya IV.

Taila II.

Taila II., then,—also called Tailapa, Nurmadi-Taila I., and A'havamalla I.,—restored the Western Chálukya dynasty and ascended the throne in Saka 895 (A.D. 973-4), the Srimukha *samvatsara*, and reigned for twenty-four years. His wife was Jákabbe, or Jákaladevi, the daughter of Kakka III., the last of the Ráshtrakuta kings. We have only four inscriptions of his time,—one at Saundatti in the Belgaum District, dated Saka 902 (A.D. 980-1), the Vikrama *samvatsara*,[1] while his feudatory, the *Mahásámanta* Sántivarmá, of the Ratta family, was governing at Sugandhavarti; another at Sogal, near Saundatti, of the same date, while his feudatory Kártavirya I., of the same family, was governing the Kundi country; the first part of an inscription at Bhairanmatti in the Kaládgi District, dated Saka 911 for 912 (A.D. 990-91), the Vikriti *samvatsara*;[2] and an inscription at Tálgund in Maisur, dated Saka 919 (A.D. 997-8), the Hemalambi *samvatsara*.[3] Where his capital was, is not clear. But,—as the third of his inscriptions is in the Kaládgi District, and as the fourth is in Maisur and records that his feudatory, Bhimarasa, also called Tailapana-Ankakára or 'the warrior or champion of Tailapa,'

---

1 *Jour. Bo. Br. R. As. Soc.*, Vol. IX., p. 204.—Sugandhavarti is the Sanskrit name of Saundatti, the chief town of the Parasgad Táluká.

2 *P. S. and O.-C. Inscriptions*, No. 86. 3 *Id.*, No. 214.

was the governor of the districts known as the Banavase Twelve-thousand and the Sántalige Thousand in Maisur, and aols the Kisukád Seventy or the country lying round Pattadakal in the Kaládgi District,—it is plain that he had then fully re-established the Chálukya sway over at least all the territories that they had held in the Kanarese districts of this Presidency. In addition to subverting the power of the Ráshtrakutas, he is said also to have overcome the king of Chedi, the Utkalas or people of Orissa, and the kings of Chola and Nepála, and to have subjugated the whole of the country of Kuntala.[1] His alleged conquest of Nepála must certainly be an invention of the poets. The other statements are perhaps true, but remain to be verified.

Satyásraya II. Taila II. was succeeded, in Saka 919 (A.D. 997-8), the Hemalambi *samvatsara*, by his eldest son Satyásraya II., also called Sattiga and Irivibhujamga. Of his time we have seven inscriptions,[2] —one at Gadag in the Dhárwád District, dated Saka 924 (A.D. 1002-3), the Subhakrit *samvatsara*, while his feudatory Sábhanarasa or Sobhanarasa was governing the districts known as the Belvola Three-hundred,[3] the Puligere or Lakshmeswar Three-hundred, and some other smaller districts; one at Kukkanur in the Nizám's Dominions, the date of which is not certain, as only the figures 9 and 2 are shown by the copyist to be legible, and the name of the *samvatsara* is illegible; one at Tumbige in the Kaládgi District, dated Saka 926 (A.D. 1004-5), the Krodhi *samvatsara*; one at Yalawál in Maisur, in the date of which, again, only the figures 9 and 2 are legible and the name of the *samvatsara* is illegible, while a feudatory of his was governing the Banavase Twelve-thousand; one at Kanneswar in the Dhárwád District, dated Saka 927 (A.D. 1005-6), the Visvávasu *samvatsara*, while his feudatory Bhimarája, also called Tailapana-

---

1 The Western Chálukyas are constantly described emphatically as the 'lords of Kuntala,' though their sway was by no means always confined to that country. The limits of Kuntala cannot at present be defined exactly. But it included, on the south, Balagámve and Harihar in Maisur, and Hampe or Vijayanagar in the Ballári District. To the north of these places, it included Lakshmeswar, Gadag, Lakkundi, and Naregal, in the Dhárwád District, and Kukkanur in the Nizám's Dominions; further to the north, Konnur, Kalhole, Saundatti, and Munawalli, in the Belgaum District, and Pattadakal and Aihole in the Kaládgi District; and further still to the north, Bijápur, Taddewádi, and Mannugulli, in the Kaládgi District. Still further to the north, it probably included Kalyána itself; but the inscriptions as yet available do not suffice to define its extent in that direction and to the north-west. In the south-west corner, again, it included Banawási in North Kanara, and Hángal in the Dhárwád District, and was bounded there by the Hayve Five-hundred, which was one of the divisions of the Konkana, and which lay between Hángal, Banawási, and Balagámve, and the coast. To the north of Hángal, the Palasige or Halsi Twelve-thousand, the Venugráma or Belgaum Seventy, and the territory of the Siláháras of Kolhápur, do not seem to have formed part of Kuntala, but, lying along the inland slopes of the Western Ghauts and being bounded on the west immediately by the Konkana, to have been treated rather as up-country divisions of the Konkana itself. The principal divisions of Kuntala were the Banavåse Twelve-thousand, Pánungal Five-hundred, Puligere Three-hundred, Belvola Three-hundred, Kundi Three-thousand, Toragale Six-thousand, Kelavádi Three-hundred, Kisukád Seventy, Bágadage Seventy, and Taddevádi Thousand.

2 Elliot *MS. Collection*, Vol. I., pp. 29 to 34; and *Ind. Ant.*, Vol. II., p. 297.

3 Belvola, from the Kanarese *bele*, 'to increase, grow; standing corn, a crop,' + *hola*, 'a field,' was the ancient name of the country surrounding and including Gadag, Lakkundi, and Dambal, in the Dhárwád District, Huli in the Belgaum District, and Kukkanur in the Nizám's Dominions. In Sanskrit passages the name is written Beluvala.

Ankakára, was still governing the Kisukád, Banavase, and Sántalige districts; the Khárepátan plates, dated Saka 930 (A.D. 1008-9), the Kilaka *samvatsara*, and containing a grant of his feudatory, Ráhurája, of the southern branch of the Siláháras of the Konkan;[1] and an inscription at Munawalli near Bankápur, dated somewhat later in the same year. The exact termination of his reign is not known; but we may adopt Sir Walter Elliot's opinion that it ended in about Saka 930 (A. D. 1008-9), the Kilaka *samvatsara*.[2]

Dasavarmá.

The next name in the list is that of Dasavarmá, the younger brother of Satyásraya II. All that we know about him is that his wife was Bhágyavati or Bhágaladevi. As there are no inscriptions of his time, and as his name is omitted in some of the later inscriptions, it is probable that he did not actually reign.

Vikramáditya V.

The actual successor of Satyásraya II., in about Saka 930 (A.D. 1008-9), the Kilaka *samvatsara*, appears to have been Vikrama or Vikramáditya V., also called Tribhuvanamalla I., the eldest son of Dasavarmá. Of his time we have three inscriptions,[3] —one at Sudi in the Dhárwád District, dated Saka 932 (A.D. 1010-1), the Sádhárana *samvatsara*; one at A'lur in the Gadag Táluká in the same District, and of the same year, while his feudatory, Iriva-Nolambádhirája, also called Ghadiya-Ankakára or Gadiya-Ankakára, was governing the Nolambavádi Thirty-two-thousand in Maisur, the Kengere Two-hundred, the Ballakundi Three-hundred, the Kukkanur Thirty, and five towns in the Másavádi country; and one at Galagnáth in the same District, dated Saka 933 (A.D. 1011-2), the Virodhikrit *samvatsara*. The termination of his reign is put by Sir Walter Elliot in about Saka 940 (A.D. 1018-9), the Kálayukti *samvatsara*.

Ayyana II.

The next name in the list is that of Ayyana II., the younger brother of Vikramáditya V. We have, however, no records of him; and he does not appear to have really reigned.

Akkádevi, and Jayasimha III.

The actual successor of Vikramáditya V., in about Saka 940 (A.D. 1018-9), the Kálayukti *samvatsara*, was his youngest brother, Jayasimha III., who also bore the titles of Jagadekamalla I. and Vallabhanarendra. His wife was Suggaladevi. Of his time we have the Miraj copper-plate grant,[4] and some twenty-four stone-tablets, ranging from Saka 940 (A.D. 1018-9) the Kálayukti *samvatsara*, to Saka 964 (A.D. 1042-3) the Chitrabhánu *samvatsara*, —at Balagámve and Tálgund in Maisur; at Kalyán, Hávanige, Benkankond, and other places, in the Dhárwád District; at Huli in the Belgaum District; at Arasibidi, Belur, Bhairanmatti, and other places more to the north, in the Kaládgi District; and at Alawandi in the Nizám's Dominions.[3] In several of them he is spoken of as defeating the Chola king. But no details are given, except in the Miraj plates, which state that the grant recorded in

1 *Jour. Bo. Br. R. As. Soc.*, Vol. I., p. 209.
2 *Madras Journal of Literature and Science*, Vol. VII., p. 196.
3 Elliot *MS. Collection*, Vol. I., pp. 37 to 40. 3 *Ind. Ant.*, Vol. VIII., p. 10.
4 Elliot *MS. Collection*, Vol. I., pp. 44 to 74; *P. S.* and *O.-C. Inscriptions*, Nos. 70, 86, 153, 154, 155, and 215; *Ind. Ant.*, Vol. IV., p. 278, and Vol. V., p. 15; and inscriptions collected by myself, as yet unpublished. From this time the inscriptions become too numerous to give the details of all of them in this paper.

them was made by him in Saka 946 (A.D. 1024-5), the Raktákshi *samvatsara*, at his victorious camp, which, after warring against the mighty Chola, the lord of the city of Chandramila, and after seizing the possessions of the lords of the seven Konkanas, was located near the city of Kollápura, the modern Kolhápur, for the purpose of conquering the northern country. His principal feudatories and officials were,—the *Mahámandalesvara* Kundamarasa, of the family of the Kádambas of Banawási and Hángal, who in Saka 941 (A.D. 1019-20) was governing the Banavâse Twelve-thousand, the Sántalige Thousand, and the Hayve Five-hundred, up to the borders of the western ocean, at the capital of Balipura or Balagámve; the *Dandanáyaka* Barmadeva, who in Saka 946 (A.D. 1024-5) was governing the Taddevádi Thousand, the Belvola Three-hundred, and the Puligere Three-hundred; the *Mahámandalesvaras* Sevya and Nágáditya, of the Sinda family, who in Saka 955 (A.D. 1033-4) were governing the Bágadage country; the *Mahámandalesvara* Mayuravarmá II., of the family of the Kádambas of Banawási and Hángal, who in Saka 956 (A.D. 1034-5), and Saka 960, was governing the Pánungal or Hángal Five-hundred; and Nolamba-Pallava-Bommanayya or Bammanayya, who in Saka 962 (A.D. 1040-1) and Saka 964 was governing five towns in the Másavádi One-hundred-and-forty. Also, the Belur inscription of Saka 944 (A.D. 1022-3) shows that his elder sister Akkádevi was entrusted with the government of the Kisukád Seventy. The Balagámve inscriptions of Saka 941 (A.D. 1019-20) and Saka 957 give that place, under its ancient name of Balligáve or Balipura, as his capital. Also, the Bhairanmatti inscription of Saka 955 (A.D. 1033-4) gives as his capital Kollipáke, a place which I cannot as yet find in the maps;[1] and the second Balagámve inscription, and one at Alawandi of the same date, give us another capital, Pottalakere,[2] which also I cannot as yet find in the maps.

---

[1] It should, however, be a very well known place, being the slightly differently spelt Kollipáki which is mentioned in the *Rájasekharavilása*, I., 53 to 56, as the birthplace of Renukesa, Renukácharya, or Revanaprabhu. According to the poem, Renukesa was born from the *isa* or *linga* at Kollipáki, into which he was absorbed again, when he had begotten a son named Rudramunisvara, and had initiated him and given him the office of *guru*. In his introduction to his edition of the *Rájasekharavilása*, Gangádhar Madiwáleswar Turmari states that Renukesa was one of the *Panchácháryas* or five preceptors who established the Lingáyat religion, and that he founded a *matha* or religious college at Kollipáki and gave the *pattádhikára* or pontiffship of it to his son Rudramunisvara;—that in Rudramunisvara's lineage were born Uddánaganádhisvara, Annadánisa, Revanasiddhesvara, and Chikkaviradeva, who established a *matha* at Danugur, south of Bengalur, and became the *svámis* or pontiffs of it;—that in Chikkaviradeva's lineage was born the poet Shadakshari, the author of the *Rájasekharavilása*, who became the *pattadasvámi* of the Danugur *matha* about A. D. 1631;—that Shadakshari died at Yelendur, in Maisur, where the people set up in memory of him a *linga* which they worship to this day;—and that his descendants are still found at Kollipáki, Danugur, and Yelendur. But he does not give any information as to where Kollipáki is to be looked for.

[2] This, again, should be a very well known place, being the slightly differently spelt Hotalakere of the *Basava-Purána*, chap. LI., in which it is said that it contained seven hundred *basadis* or Jain temples and twenty thousand Jain saints, and the subject of which is how Devara-Dásimayya, the *guru* of Suggaladevi the wife of king Desinga, despoiled the *Srávakas* or Jains and induced Desinga to adopt the Saiva or Lingáyat religion. The same story is epitomised in the *Channabasava-Purána*, LVII., 10, which says that Suggale, the wife of the *Jinabhakta* Desinga-Ballála, caused her *guru* Devara-Dása to dispute with the Jains, and then, transforming a serpent in a box into a *linga* made of the *chandrakánta* or moon-stone, she

Jayasimha III. was succeeded, in or about Saka 964 (A.D. 1042-3) the Chitrabhánu *samvatsara*, by his son Somesvara I., also called Trailokyamalla I. and A'havamalla II. Of his time we have some forty inscriptions, ranging from Saka 966 (A.D. 1042-3), the Tárana *samvatsara*, to Saka 990 (A.D. 1068-9), the Kilaka *samvatsara*,—at Tálgund, Balagámve, and Dávangere, in Maisur; at Banawási in North Kanara; at Nilgund, A'dur, Ingalgondi, and other places, in the Dhárwád District; at Saundatti in the Belgaum District; at Arasibidi and Devur, in the Kaládgi District; and at Talakal, Kembhávi, and other places in the Nizám's Dominions.[1] His wives were Báchaladevi,[2] Chandalakabbe or Chandrikádevi,[3] and Mailaladevi.[4] His principal feudatories and officials were,—the *Mahámandalesvara* Mayuravarmá II., of the family of the Kádambas of Banawási and Hángal, who in Saka 966 (A.D. 1044-5) was governing the Pánungal Five-hundred; the *Mahámandalesvara* Chávundaráya, of the same family, who in Saka 967 (A.D. 1045-6) and Saka 984 (A.D. 1062-3) was governing the Banavase Twelve-thousand at his capital of Balligáve or Balagámve; the *Mahásámantas* Kártavirya I. and Anka, of the Ratta family, the latter of whom in Saka 971 (A.D. 1049-50), was governing at Sugandhavarti in the Kundi Three-thousand; and the *Mahámandalesvara* Kirttivarmá II., of the family of the Kádambas of Banawási and Hángal, who in Saka 990 (A.D. 1068-9) was governing the Banavase Twelve-thousand. Also his aunt, Akkádevi, continued in authority during his reign; for, in one of the Arasibidi inscriptions, of Saka 969 (A.D. 1047-8), we find her laying siege to the fort of Gokáge, which can only be Gokák in the Belgaum District, probably to quell some local insurrection. Also we find that in Saka 975 (A.D. 1053-4) his wife Mailaladevi, who is called the *piriy-arasi*, or 'chief queen', was entrusted with the government of the Banavase Twelve-thousand; that in Saka 971 (A.D. 1049-50) and Saka 975 his eldest son Somesvara II., also called Gangapermánadi[5] - Bhuvanaikavira, was governing the Belvola Three-hundred and the Puligere Three-hundred; and that in Saka 977 (A.D. 1055-6) his second son Gangapermánadi-Vikrama, or Vikramáditya VI., was governing the Gangavádi Ninety-six-thousand in Maisur and the Banavase Twelve-thousand, with Harikesari, of the family of the Kádambas of Banawási and Hángal, as his subordinate in charge of the latter district.[6] It is

Somesvara I.

---

caused him to conquer, and induced her husband to become a *Sivabhakta*. The *Channabasava-Purána* calls Desinga a Ballála, *i.e.* a Hoysala; but this is evidently a mistake. Desinga is a corruption of Jayasimha; and the coincidence of the other names of Suggale or Suggaladevi, and Hotalakere, shows conclusively that the story really refers to the Western Chálukya king Jayasimha III., whose wife was Suggaladevi, and one of whose capitals was Pottalakere.

1 Elliot *MS. Collection*, Vol. I., pp. 77 to 195; *P. S.* and *O.-C. Inscriptions*, Nos. 92, 136, 156, 157, 158, and 216; *Ind. Ant.*, Vol. IV., p. 179; and unpublished inscriptions.

2 *Ind. Ant.*, Vol. II., p. 297.

3 Elliot *MS. Collection*, Vol. I., p. 92.

4 *Id.*, Vol. I., p. 122.

5 This title, belonging to both Somesvara II. and Vikramáditya VI., indicates that their mother was of the Ganga family. The mother of Jayasimha IV., on the other hand, must have been a Pallava princess.

6 *Ind. Ant.*, Vol. IV., p. 203.—In this inscription, in addition to being called Gangapermánadi, Vikramáditya VI. has the other Ganga titles of Satyavákya-Konguṇivarma-Dharmamahárájádhirája, Kuvalála-puravar-esvara, Nandagiri-nátha, Madagajendra-lánchhana, Padmávati-labdha-varaprasáda, Ganga-Kusumáyudha, and Nanniya-Ganga.—He must at this time have been very young, and the government of the two provinces in question probably was actually carried on by his mother in his name.

in the time of this king, and in Saka 975 (A.D. 1053-4), that we first find Kalyána mentioned as a Western Chálukya capital.[1] How the mistake arose, I do not know; but it is not an uncommon thing to find the Early and Western Chalukyas called 'the Chalukyas of Kalyánapura.' This is nothing but a complete error. Kalyána is nowhere mentioned in the Early and Western Chalukya inscriptions; and, even if it existed as a city at that time, it certainly was not a Chalukya capital. The earliest mention of it is the one that I have just pointed out; and it was probably not long, if at all, before Saka 975 that it fell into the hands of the Western Chálukyas, who were then in the course of reconquering the ancient dominions of their ancestors towards the north. We find, from an inscription of his eldest son and successor,[2] that in the time of Somesvara I. the Chola king made an incursion into the Western Chálukya dominions. He invaded the Belvola Three-hundred and burnt many temples there, and then proceeded to Puligere, or Lakshmeswar, and destroyed the Jain temples which had been built by Permádiganga. This incursion was probably by way of retaliation for the defeat which he himself had experienced at the hands of Jayasimha III. The success of the Cholas, however, did not last long. Somesvara I. repulsed them, and drove them back southwards, and the leader of the Cholas lost his life in a battle which was fought apparently at the city of Kakkaragond, on the bank of the Tungabhadrá; Sir Walter Elliot identifies this place with Kakargudi, a small village on the south bank of the river, between Harihar and Dávangere. This victory over the Cholas is also referred to in one of the inscriptions of Somesvara I. himself,[3] which records that, —having conquered the region of the south, and having defeated the Chola king,—on the occasion of an eclipse of the moon on Monday the day of the full-moon of the month Mágha of Saka 981 (A.D. 1059-60), the Vikári *samvatsara,* while he was encamped at Puliyapaina [4] in the Siddhavádi country, he gave the village of Sivanur, in the Kisukád Seventy, by a copper-plate grant, to Somesvarapandita, the priest of the god Nágesvara of the shrine of the god Nagaresvara at the capital of Sundi. This conquest of the Cholas is recorded also in the *Vikramánkadevacharita* of Bilhana, [5] which states that Somesvara I. penetrated as far as Kánchi itself, stormed it, and drove its ruler into the jungles. The same chronicle also states that he stormed Dhárá, the capital

---

1 *Ind. Ant.*, Vol. VIII., p. 105.

2 Elliot *MS. Collection*, Vol. I., p. 216.—The date of this inscription is Saka 993 (A.D. 1071-72), the Virodhikrit *samvatsara*,—the date being expressed by the words *guna* or the 3 qualities, *labdha* or the 9 units, and *randhra* or the 9 orifices of the body,—the order of which is to be inverted in reading them off, according to the rule *ankánám vámato gatih*. This is the earliest instance known to me of a date being thus expressed by numerical words.

3 Elliot *MS. Collection*, Vol. I., p. 144.

4 It is written so in the copy. But Mr. Rice (*Mysore Inscriptions*, p. lxiv.) adopts the form of Puliyarpattana, and identifies it with the modern Huliyar in the Chitaldurg District. He also, as well as Sir Walter Elliot, identifies Sivanur with the modern Sávanur, near Bankápur in the Dhárwád District. But Sivanur cannot be in that direction at all. It is, perhaps, the modern 'Seewoopoor' of the maps, about three miles south of Bádámi; this, at any rate, is the neighbourhood in which it is to be looked for.

5 I., 114 to 117.

of the Pramáras in Málava, from which king Bhoja had to flee;[1] that he utterly destroyed the power of Karna, king of Dáhala,[2] *i.e.* Karna, the son of Gángeya, of the family of the Kalachuris of Tripura or Tewar;[3] and that he beautified Kalyána so that it surpassed in splendour all the other cities of the earth.[4] In the genealogy at page 17 above, I have given the names of three sons of Somesvara I.,—*viz.* Somesvara II., Vikramáditya VI., and Jayasimha IV. The Dávangere inscription of Saka 988 (A. D. 1066-7), the Parábhava *samvatsara*,[5] purports to give the name of a fourth son, the *Mahárája* Vishnuvardhana-Vijayáditya,—also called A'havamallana-Ankakára, and Sáhasamalla,—who was then governing the Nolambavádi Thirty-two-thousand in Maisur, and by whose *Dandanáyaka* and *Mahásandhivigrahi* Devapayya the grants recorded in the inscription were made. There is no reason for refusing to accept this inscription as genuine; and it certainly speaks of Vishnuvardhana-Vijayáditya as the son[6] of Somesvara I. But he is mentioned in no other inscription as yet known. Now, the name of Vijayáditya does occur once in this family, in the seventh century A. D., in the case of the son of Vinayáditya; but it is not repeated after that among the Western Chalukyas and Chálukyas, though, in later times, it was the name of several members of the Eastern Branch. Again, Vishnuvardhana was a frequent enough name among the Eastern Chalukyas, but does not occur once in the Western Branch, except in the case of Vishnuvardhana I., the younger brother of Pulikesi II., who separated from the Western Chalukyas and founded the Eastern Branch; and it is a name that would not be at all likely to be chosen for any member of the Western Chálukya dynasty, which made no particular profession of the worship of Vishnu. Finally, this Vishnuvardhana-Vijayáditya had the title of *Vengimandalesvara*, or 'lord of the province of Vengi,' which, as is well known, was the hereditary territory of the Eastern Chalukyas and their Chola successors. That Vishnuvardhana-Vijayáditya was a person of considerable rank and position, is shown by his being called a *Mahárája*,—by his having so high a minister as a *Mahásandhivigrahi*,—and by his being in charge of so large a province as the Nolambavádi Thirty-two-thousand. And, that he was of Chálukya extraction, is shown by his also having in this inscription the title of *Chálukya-mánikya*, or 'the ruby of the Chálukyas.' But I am disposed to consider that he was not really the son of Somesvara I., but,—being a connection of his through the female line, in the next degree of descent after him, in the family of the Chola successors of the Eastern Chalukyas; and being raised by him to a position of great authority, in fact to that of viceroy of a large province,—he was simply called the son of Somesvara I. through

Vishnuvardhana-Vijayáditya.

---

1 I., 91 to 96. This is probably the Bhoja, who is referred to in also the time of Jayasimha III. (*Ind. Ant.*, Vol. V., p. 17).

2 I., 102, 103.

3 See General Cunningham's *Archæological Reports*, Vol. IX., pp. 85 and 107.

4 *Vikramánkadevacharita*, II., 1 to 25.

5 *P. S. and O.-C. Inscriptions*, No. 136.

6 *Tan-nandana*, I. 6. It may be noted, however, that the inscription does not make use of any such expression as *átange puttida*, 'born to him.'

courtesy.[1] I have, therefore, not given him a place in the Western Chálukya genealogy.

Somesvara II.

Somesvara I. was succeeded, in or about Saka 990 (A.D. 1068-9), the Kilaka *samvatsara*, by his eldest son, Somesvara II., also called Bhuvanaikamalla, who reigned up to Saka 997 (A.D. 1075-6), the Rákshasa *samvatsara*. Of his time we have some twenty inscriptions, ranging from Saka 991 (A.D. 1069-70), the Saumya *samvatsara*, to Saka 997 (A.D. 1075-76), the Rákshasa *samvatsara*,—at Balagámve, Kuppatur, and A'nawatti, in Maisur; at Sudi, Soratur, Gawarawád, Kallukeri, and Gudugudi, in the Dhárwád District; at Huli, Kádarawalli, and Saundatti, in the Belgaum District; at Arasibidi and Bijápur in the Kaládgi District; and at Antaratáni in the Nizám's Dominions.[2] His principal feudatories and officials were,—Lakshmarasa, who in Saka 993 (A.D. 1071-72) was governing the Belvola Three-hundred and the Puligere Three-hundred, and who repaired the Jain temples which the Cholas had destroyed in the reign of Somesvara I.; Udayáditya, of the Ganga family, who in Saka 993 was governing at the city of Bankápura, and in Saka 997 (A.D. 1075-76) was governing the Banavase Twelve-thousand, the Sántalige Thousand, the Mandali Thousand, and the Eighteen *Agraháras*;[3] the *Dandanáyaka* Nákimayya, who in Saka 996 (A.D. 1074-75) was governing the Taddevádi Thousand; and the *Mahámandalesvara* Kártavirya II., of the Ratta family, who was governing at Sugandhavarti. The principal capital of Somesvara II. seems to have been Kalyána. His reign was a short one and apparently of no importance, for his inscriptions contain no historical information, except that Udayáditya is said to have conquered for him the Chera, Chola, Pándya, and Pallava kings, and others who dwelt on his frontiers, and to have levied tribute from them. In the end he appears to have alienated the affections of his subjects, by tyranny or by neglect, and thus to have led to his dethronement by his younger brother Vikramáditya VI., who "by the strength of his own arm seized upon the recent sovereignty of Bhuvanaikamalla."[4]

Vikramáditya VI.

Vikramáditya VI.,—who was more commonly called Tribhuvanamalla II., and who also bore the names of Permádi, Kalivikrama,

---

1 This is a very common custom in the Kanarese country. When a witness in Court speaks of such and such a man as being his son or his brother, it is always necessary, if the point is at all relevant, to make him explain whether he means, in the first case, his own son, his brother's son, or the son of a distant relative in the same degree of descent with himself, and, in the second case, his own father's son, his uncle's son, or the son of a distant relative in the same degree of descent with his father; and so with some other relationships also.—In the inscriptions we have an instance of this in *P. S. and O.-C. Inscriptions*, No. 180, where Jayakesi II., of the Kádambas of Goa, is called the elder brother (*nij-ágrajáta* ; l. 23) of Jagaddeva, of the Sántara kings of Patti-Pombuchchapura in Maisur, and Jagaddeva is called the younger brother (*priy-ánuja* ; l. 27) of Jayakesi. A somewhat more correct expression is used in l. 19 of the inscription, *viz.* that Jayakesi "was *considered to be* the younger brother" of Jagaddeva (*agrajanman = enisidan*). Jayakesi II. and Jagaddeva were really maternal cousins, being the sons of two sisters, Chattaladevi and Bijjaladevi.

2 Elliot *MS. Collection*, Vol. I., pp. 199 to 250; and *P. S. and O.-C. Inscriptions*, Nos. 92, 159, 160, 161, and 162.

3 The Eighteen *Agraháras* appear to have been, not a collection of eighteen contiguous townships, but eighteen towns of importance scattered over the eastern parts of the kingdom. Huli, in the Belgaum District, was one of them; and perhaps Dambal in the Dhárwád District was another.

4 Elliot *MS. Collection*, Vol. I., pp. 370 and 415.

Vikramárka and Vikramánka,—ascended the throne on Monday the fifth day of the bright fortnight of the month Phálguna of Saka 997 (A.D. 1073-4), the Rákshasa *samvatsara,* and reigned till Saka 1048 (A.D. 1126-7), the Parábhava *samvatsara.*[1] One of the first acts of his reign was to abolish the use of the original Saka era, and to supersede it by a new era established in his own name. As the inscriptions say,—"Having said, 'Why should the glory of the kings Vikramáditya and Nanda be a hindrance any longer?' he, with a loudly uttered command, abolished that *(era)* which has the name of Saka, and made that *(era)* which has the Chálukya figures;"—and again, "Having slain all the hostile kings, by his amplitude and alone, Tribhuvanamalla, the king Chálukya-Vikramáditya, became the favourite of the world. Having rubbed out the brilliant *Sakavarsha,* he, the impetuous one, the most liberal man in the world, who delighted in religion, published his name throughout the world under the form of the *Vikramakála.*"[2] I have not found any instance of this era having been adopted by the kings of other dynasties; but nearly all the inscriptions of his own time, and a few of his successors, are dated in the Chálukya-Vikramakála or Chálukya-Vikramavarsha, thus established by him, which commenced from the date of his coronation as given above. And, in determining the chronological order of his inscriptions, it must be borne in mind that, as the result of the initial date of this era being so close to the initial date of the years of the Saka era, the *samvatsaras* of the sixty-years cycle were made to commence and end with the years of his era, instead of with the years of the Saka era as had been the case up to then. Of his time there are already known to exist nearly two hundred inscriptions, containing an enormous amount of materials which still remain to be properly digested and arranged.[3] And, being scattered over the northern parts of Maisur, the eastern parts of North Kanara, the whole of the Dhárwád, Belgaum, and Kaládgi Districts, and the western and north-western parts of the Nizám's Dominions, they show very clearly the large and universal extent of his kingdom and sway in this part of the country. Also General Cunningham has found one of his inscriptions on an elaborately sculptured pillar at Sitabaldi near Nágpur in the Central Provinces. It is dated Saka 1009 (A.D. 1087-8); and another of his inscriptions tells us that in Saka 1020 (A.D. 1098-99) he was still in the north and was then on the banks of the Narmadá.[4] One of the most interesting of his inscriptions is the Buddhist tablet at Dambal,[5] which records grants made to a *vihára* of Buddha and a *vihára* of A'rya-Tárádevi at that town, in Saka 1017 (A.D. 1095-6), and which thus shows that the Buddhist religion still held a place in the Kanarese country as late as the end of the eleventh century A.D. He indulged in a pretty considerable plurality of wives; I have found the names of the following seven mentioned,—Málaladevi or Málikaráni, the daughter of the *Sánabhoga* or hereditary village-

---

1 *Ind. Ant.*, Vol. VIII., pp. 189 and 193.
2 *Id.*, Vol. VIII., p. 187.
3 Elliot *MS. Collection*, Vol. I., pp. 255 to 672; *P. S. and O.-C. Inscriptions*, Nos. 82, 88, 90, 103, 108, 113, 137, 138, 163 to 177, 217, and 218; and unpublished inscriptions.
4 Elliot *MS. Collection*, Vol. I., p. 92.
5 *Ind. Ant.*, Vol. X., pp. 185 and 273.

accountant, Ráyanna, of Yelawatti; Sávaladevi, the daughter of Jogamarána or Jogamarasa and Táradevi of the Suryavamsa; Chandaladevi, the mother of Jayakarna; Jakkaladevi; Malleyamadevi or Malayamatidevi; Lakshmádevi, who in Saka 1017 (A.D. 1095-96), was governing at Dharmápura or Dharmavolal, the modern Dambal in the Dhárwád District; and Engaladevi.[1] Of these, Chandaladevi, also called Chandralekhá, was the daughter of one of the Siláhára *Mahámandalesvaras* of Kolhápur; and one of his wives was a daughter of the Chola king.[2] The foundation of his power, and of his popularity with his subjects which led to his so easily usurping the sovereignty from his elder brother, appears to have been laid in the time of his father Somesvara I., when he was invested with the authority of viceroy at Banawási, as we have already seen; and when he was also employed to command many successful expeditions, in which he is said to have repeatedly defeated the Cholas, and plundered Kánchi,—to have lent his assistance to the king of Málava, who sought his aid to regain his kingdom, and to have carried his arms as far north as Gauda and Kámarupa,—to have attacked the king of Simhala or Ceylon,—to have destroyed the sandalwood forests of the Malaya hills,—to have slain the king of Kerala,—and to have conquered the cities of Gángakunda, Vengi, and Chakrakota or Chakragotta.[3] His first idea seems to have been to leave his elder brother Somesvara II. in possession of part of the kingdom at Kalyána, and to have set up an independency of his own at Banawási; and it was probably with the object of strengthening his hands in that direction, that he gave his daughter Mailaladevi in marriage to Jayakesi II., of the family of the Kádambas of Goa.[4] Subsequent events, however, interfered with this plan. A rebellion occurred in the Chola dominions, in the course of which his brother-in-law was killed, and Rájiga, the king of Vengi, took possession of Kánchi. Vikramáditya marched to the south to meet Rájiga, and Somesvara II. followed with another army, promising outwardly to assist his brother, but intending secretly to play the traitor. A battle ensued, in which Rájiga fled and Somesvara was taken prisoner, and Vikramáditya VI. then proclaimed himself monarch of all the Western Chálukya dominions.[5] His long reign was a fairly peaceful one, except that his younger brother Jayasimha IV., whom he had made his viceroy at Banawási, created a rebellion, and, winning over many of the local chieftains, advanced as far as the river Krishná; but a battle was fought, in which Jayasimha was made captive, and the insurrection was easily crushed.[6] The chief capital of Vikramáditya VI. was Kalyána; but he had also a capital at Etagiri, the modern Yátagiri in the western parts of the Nizám's Dominions;[7] and he also either built or greatly enlarged Arasibidi in the Kaládgi District, and made it another of his capitals under the name of Vikramapura. The most important of his feudatories and officials were, — the *Mahámandalesvara*

---

1 Elliot *MS. Collection*, Vol. I., pp. 276, 305, 339, 344, 353, 356, 415, 422, 448, 451, 491, 527, and 616.

2 *Vikramánkadevacharita*, V. 79.

3 *Id.*, Introd., p. 31.

4 *Jour. Bo. Br. R. As. Soc.*, Vol. IX., p. 232.

5 *Vikramánkadevacharita*, Introd., pp. 35 to 37.

6 *Id.*, pp. 42, 43.

7 *Ind. Ant.*, Vol. IX., p. 50; Lat. 16° 46′ N., Long. 77° 13′ E.

Kirttivarmá II., of the family of the Kádambas of Banawási and Hángal, who in Saka 998 (A.D. 1076-77) and Saka 999 was governing the Banavase Twelve-thousand; the *Mahápradhána* and *Dandanáyaka* Barmadeva, who in Saka 999 (A.D. 1077-78) was governing the Banavase Twelve-thousand and the Eighteen *Agraháras*; the *Mahámandalesvara* Sántivarmá II., of the family of the Kádambas of Banawási and Hángal, who in Saka 1010 (A. D. 1088-89) was governing the Banavase Twelve-thousand and the Pánungal Five-hundred; the *Mahámandalesvara* Tailapa II., of the same family, who in Saka 1021 (A. D. 1099-1100), Saka 1030, and Saka 1037, was governing the Banavåse Twelve-thousand and the Pánungal Five-hundred; the *Mahámandalesvaras* Kanna II., Sena II., and Kártavirya II., of the Ratta family, who were governing at Sugandhavarti; the *Mahápradhána* and *Dandanáyaka* Anantapála, who in Saka 1025 (A.D. 1103-4) was governing the Belvola Three-hundred, the Puligere Three-hundred, and the Banavase Twelve-thousand; the *Mahápradhána*, *Dandanáyaka*, and *Manevergade* or chamberlain, Govinda, who in Saka 1036 (A.D. 1114-15) was governing the Banavase Twelve-thousand and the Sántalige Thousand; Tribhuvanamalla-Pándyadeva, who in Saka 1043 (A.D. 1121-12) was governing the Nonambavádi Thirty-two-thousand in Maisur; and the *Mahámandalesvara* A'chugi II., of the Sinda family of Erambarage, who in Saka 1044 (A.D. 1122-3) was governing the Kisukád Seventy, the Kelavádi Three-hundred, the Bágadage Seventy, and the Nareyangal Twelve. In the time of A'chugi II., there was an invasion of the Western Chálukya kingdom by the Hoysalas, who were growing into power under Vishnuvardhana, but it was successfully resisted by A'chugi, who is said also to have fought with and put to flight the Pándyas, to have taken and burnt Gove or Goa, and to have seized upon the Konkana. The Siláháras of Kolhápur, also, appear to have given some trouble about this time; as A'chugi II. is described as swallowing up and then vomiting forth a certain Bhoja who had invaded his country and who must be the first of that name in the Siláhára family. Vikramáditya VI. ceased to reign, as I have said, in Saka 1048 (A.D. 1126-7), by which time he must have been of a good old age; but he does not seem to have died for some little while after that, as there is an inscription of Saka 1054 (A.D. 1132-3), the preamble of which speaks of him as if he was then still alive.[1]

Jayasimha IV.

Jayasimha IV. was, as we have seen, his elder brother's viceroy at Banawási; but he does not seem to have survived Vikramáditya VI., and he certainly did not ascend the Western Chálukya throne. He is not often mentioned in the inscriptions. But one at Anantpur in Maisur[2] records that in Saka 1001 (A.D. 1079-80), the Siddhárthi *samvatsara*, he was governing the Banavåse Twelve-thousand; and another at Lakshmeswar records that in Saka 1003 (A.D. 1081-2), the Durmati *samvatsara*, he was governing the same province, and also the Sántalige Thousand, the Kandur Thousand, the Puligere Three-hundred, and the Belvola Three-hundred. In these two inscriptions he is called the *Yuvarája*, and has the titles of Annana

---

1 *Ind. Ant.*, Vol. VIII., p. 193.

2 *Mysore Inscriptions*, p. 305.

Ankakára, Trailokyamalla II., Vira-Nolamba, and Pallava-Permánadi. In both of them he is called *Chálukya-chudámani*, or 'the crest-jewel of the Chálukyas'. But he is also said to be *Pallavánvaya*, or 'of Pallava descent'; and this, together with his titles of Vira-Nolamba and Pallava-Permánadi, shows that his mother was a Pallava princess, and that consequently he was only the half-brother of Somesvara II. and Vikramáditya VI.

Jayakarna.

So also Jayakarna, who appears to have been the senior son of Vikramáditya VI., in virtue of his mother's rank as *agramahishi* or 'chief queen,' if not by actual priority of birth, seems, from the Ratta inscriptions and others, to have been entrusted with the authority of viceroy in the north-west parts of his father's dominions; but there is no subsequent mention of him, and he must have died before his father.

Somesvara III.

The actual successor of Vikramáditya VI., therefore, was his second son Somesvara III., also called Bhulokamalla and Sarvajna-chakravarti. He ascended the throne in Saka 1048 (A.D. 1126-7), the Parábhava *samvatsara*, and reigned till Saka 1060 (A.D. 1138-9), the Kálayukti *samvatsara*. Of his time we have about twenty inscriptions,—at Balagámve and Dávangere in Maisur; at Abbalur, Hire-Kerur, Bankápur, and other places in the Dhárwád District; at Chiknád in the Kaládgi District; and at Gobbur, Hire-Muddanur, and Nimbarigi in the Nizám's Dominions.[1] None of them record any campaigns made by him, and his reign seems in fact to have been a very tranquil one. His capital, throughout the whole of it, was Kalyána. His principal feudatories and officials were,—the *Mahámandalesvara* Permádi, of the Kalachuri family, who in Saka 1050 (A.D. 1128-9) was governing the Taddevadi country; the *Mahámandalesvara* Jayakesi II., of the family of the Kádambas of Goa, who, about Saka 1050 (A.D. 1128-9), was governing the Konkana Nine-hundred, the Palasige or Halsi Twelve-thousand, and the Venugráma or Belgaum Seventy; the *Mahámandalesvara* Mayuravarmá III., of the family of the Kádambas of Banawási and Hángal, who in Saka 1053 (A.D. 1131-2) was governing the Banavase Twelve-thousand, the Sántalige Thousand, and the Pánungal Five-hundred; Tailapa II., of the same family, who in Saka 1057 (A.D. 1135-6) was governing the Banavase Twelve-thousand, the Pánungal Five-hundred, and the Puligere Three-hundred; the *Dandanáyaka* Mahádeva, who in Saka 1060 (A.D. 1138-9) was governing at his capital of Puligere; and Virapándyadeva, who about the same time was governing the Nonambavádi Thirty-two-thousand, from his residence at the hill-fort of Uchchangidurga.

Jagadekamalla II.

Somesvara III. was succeeded, in Saka 1060 (A.D. 1138-9), the Kálayukti *samvatsara*, by his eldest son, whose real name does not appear in any of the inscriptions, and who is known only by his title of Jagadekamalla II. We have some forty-five inscriptions of his time,—at Balagámve, Harihar, and other places in Maisur; at Hire-Kerur, Bálehalli, and other places in the Dhárwád District;

[1] Elliot *MS. Collection*, Vol. I., pp. 679 to 737; and *P. S. and O.-C. Inscriptions*, Nos. 139, 178, and 179.

at Bádámi, Nálwatwád, and other places in the Kaládgi District; at Ráyabag in the Kolhápur State; and at Kukkanur, Raichur, and other places in the Nizám's Dominions.[1] Kalyána was his chief capital throughout his reign; but in Saka 1070 (A.D. 1148-9) he appears to have had also a minor capital at Kadalipura in the Kondarate Seventy, which district was on the Dhárwád and North Kanara frontiers, near Hángal.[2] His principal feudatories and officials were,—the *Dandanáyaka* Bommanayya, who in Saka 1065 (A.D. 1143-4) was governing the Banavase Twelve-thousand; the *Mahámandalesvara* Kártavirya III., of the Ratta family, who in the same year was governing the Kundi Three-thousand; the *Mahámandalesvara* Permádi I., also called Jagadekamalla-Permádi, of the Sinda family, who in Saka 1066 (A.D. 1144-5) was governing the Kisukád Seventy, the Bágadage Seventy, the Kelavádi Three-hundred, and the Nareyangal Twelve; the *Dandanáyaka* Kesirája or Kesimayya, who in Saka 1069 (A.D. 1147-8) was governing the Belvola Three-hundred, the Palasige Twelve-thousand, and the Pánungal Five-hundred; and Jagaddeva, of the family of the Sántara kings of Pombuchchapura or the modern Hombucha or Humcha in the Nagar District in Maisur.[3] It also appears that Bijjana or Bijjala, of the Kalachuri family, in subordination to whom Vijayapándyadeva was entrusted with the government of the Nonambavádi Thirty-two-thousand, was a contemporary of his; but whether he was then an independent chieftain, or was a feudatory of Jagadekamalla, is not clear. He seems, therefore, to have pretty well held together the dominions that had come down to him. But, at the same time, not altogether without opposition. For the Sinda inscriptions show that in his reign there was another invasion from the south by the Hoysala kings, under Bittiga or Vishnuvardhana; they were, however, repulsed by Permádi I., who pursued Vishnuvardhana to his capital of Dhorasamudra and besieged him there, and also captured his city of Belápura. Also the Kádambas of Goa gave some trouble; but they, again, were successfully met by Permádi I.

Jagadekamalla was succeded, in Saka 1072 (A.D. 1150-1), the Pramoda *samvatsara*, by his younger brother Taila III., also called Nurmadi-Taila II., and Trailokyamalla III. His inscriptions, of which we have only eleven, are to be found at Balagámve, Bhárangi, and Harihar in Maisur; at Pura, Hamsabhávi, and Háveri, in the Dhárwád District; at Pattadakal in the Kaládgi District; and at Taila III.

1 Elliot *MS. Collection*, Vol. I., pp. 739 to 856; and *P. S. and O.-C. Inscriptions*, Nos. 44, 119, 146, and 180.

2 Kadalipura is mentioned in an inscription at Bálehalli in the Hángal Táluká (Elliot *MS. Collection*, Vol. I., p. 825), and must be Bálehalli itself. Bálehalli, 'the village of plantains,' would be rendered in Sanskrit by Kadalipura. And it is so rendered in the case of Bálehalli, near Honnur in the Maledesa, or hill country, at which, Mr. Kittel says (*Nágavarmá's Canarese Prosody*, Introd., pp. xlviii., lxviii., and lxix.), is the *guru's* throne of the present Revanasiddha, the disciple-descendant of the Revanaprabhu or Renukácharya mentioned at p. 44, note 1, above.

3 Jagaddeva's mother was Bijjaladevi, whose sister, Chattaladevi, was married to Vijayáditya I. of the family of the Kádambas of Goa. In his early years he seems to have been held in check by the Hoysala kings Ballála I. and Vishnuvardhana. But we find him afterwards, in Saka 1071 (A.D. 1149-50), governing at Setu, which Mr. Rice thinks was in Kanara (*Mysore Inscriptions*, p. lxviii.) and coming to Balagámve and making a grant there (*P. S. and O.-C. Inscriptions*, No. 180). And he also, apparently as the feudatory of Taila III., laid siege to Anumakonda, in the time of Prola, the father of Rudradeva (*Ind. Ant.*, Vol. XI., p. 10).

Kukkanur, Kembhávi, and Harasur, in the Nizám's Dominions.[1] His capital, at any rate up to Saka 1079 (A.D. 1157-8), was Kalyána. His inscriptions give very few historical details. They mention, as his principal feudatories and officials,—the *Dandanáyaka* Mahádeva, who, in Saka 1074 (A.D. 1152-3), was governing the Puligere Three-hundred and the Banavase Twelve-thousand; and the *Mahámandalesvara* Chávunda II., of the Sinda family, who up to Saka 1085 (A.D. 1173-4) was governing the usual Sinda territories. They also mention, as his commander-in-chief, the *Mahámandalesvara* Bijjala, of the Kalachuri family; and, as the Kalachuri inscriptions subsequently record that Bijjala destroyed all the Chálukya kings and acquired the whole of the Kuntala country, it is plain that he abused the trust reposed in him, and used his sovereign's own armies to deprive the latter of his kingdom. The date of this event is fixed,—as lying somewhere between the day of the new-moon of the month Pausha of Saka 1083 (A.D. 1161-2), the Vishu *samvatsara*, and the same day in the following year, the Chitrabhánu *samvatsara*,—by two inscriptions at Balagámve [2] and at Annigeri:[3] in the former of them, Bijjala still styles himself only a *Mahámandalesvara*; while in the latter of them, he is invested with the usual regal titles of *samastabhuvanásraya*, *prithivivallabha*, *mahárájádhirája*, and *paramesvara*, and Annigeri is called the *rájadháni-pattana* or 'royal capital.' But Taila's downfall was not accomplished solely by the Kalachuris, but was aided by an attack from another powerful king from the east. An inscription at Anamkond near Worangal in the Nizám's Dominions,[4] of the Kákatya or Kákatiya king Rudradeva, tells us that Rudradeva's father, Prolarája, "in an instant made captive in war the glorious Tailapadeva, the ornament of the Chálukyas, who was skilled in the practice of riding upon elephants,—whose inmost thoughts were ever intent upon war,—and who was mounted upon an elephant which was like a cloud (*in size*); and then at once he, who was renowned in the rite of severing the throats of his (*captive*) enemies, let him go, from goodwill produced by his devotion." The same inscription records that Taila III. subsequently died in the time of Rudradeva; and,—as it is dated on the thirteenth day of the bright fortnight of the month Mágha of Saka 1084 (A.D. 1162-3), the Chitrabhánu *samvatsara*, subsequently to the overthrow of a certain king Bhima, who, on Taila's death, ventured to assume the sovereignty over a part, evidently the more eastern and northern portions, of his dominions,—it is plain that the death of Taila III. must have occurred some months before that.

Somesvara IV.

The Western Chálukya power, however, was not yet entirely destroyed. After the death of Taila III., a period of interruption of the power of the dynasty ensued. As recorded in one of the inscriptions of his son and successor, Somesvara IV., also called Soma, Vira-Somesvara, and Tribhuvanamalla III.,—the Chálukya dominions were meanwhile held by the Kalachuris. But in Saka

---

1 Elliot *MS. Collection*, Vol. II., pp. 1 to 20; and *P. S. and O.-C. Inscriptions*, Nos. 120 and 181.

2 Elliot *MS. Collection*, Vol. II., p. 67; and *P. S. and O.-C., Inscriptions*, No. 184.

3 Elliot *MS. Collection*, Vol. II., p. 72.

4 *Ind. Ant.*, Vol. X., p. 9.

1104 (A.D. 1182-3), the Subhakrit *samvatsara*,—taking advantage of the fact that, owing to the religious dissensions between the Lingáyats and the Jains at Kalyána, which they had made their capital, the power of the Kalachuris was rapidly waning, and in fact was already almost at an end,—he succeeded in re-establishing for a short time longer the semblance of a Chálukya sovereignty. He owed his power, such as it was, to the influence and energy of his *Dandanáyaka* Barmarasa, who in one of his inscriptions is called *Chálukya-rájya-pratisthápaka*, or 'the establisher of the Chálukya sovereignty.' This person is evidently the same Barmarasa who in Saka 1083 (A.D. 1161-2) was the *Dandanáyaka* of Bijjala and had the government of the Banavásе province under him, while Bijjala was still, nominally, if not actually, only the commander-in-chief of Taila III.,—and also the Brahmá, *i.e.* Barma, the general in command of the Kalachuri army, by defeating whom the Hoysalas, under Ballála II., first established their power north of the Tungabhadrá. This defeat destroyed the power of the Kalachuris. But the Hoysalas found too much to occupy them in the eastern parts of the kingdom to admit of their making at once an attack in the direction of Banawási, which was not permanently in their possession till Saka 1114 (A.D. 1192-3). And Barmarasa evidently took advantage of this to fall back on Banawási, and there espouse the cause and fortunes of the son of his former sovereign Taila III. Somesvara IV. made Annigeri,[1] in the Dhárwád District, his capital. And, his inscriptions being found only at Annigeri, Dambal, Lakkundi, Hángal, Kallukeri, Neregal in the Hángal Táluká, and Ablur, in the Dhárwád District,[2] the limited extent of his rule is apparent. His inscriptions contain no historical details. His principal feudatories and officials were,—the *Mahápradhána* and *Dandanáyaka* Tejimayya, who in Saka 1106 (A.D. 1184-5) was governing at Dharmápura or Dambal in the Másavádi country; the *Dandanáyaka* Barmarasa, who in the same year was governing at the capital of Annigeri; the *Mahápradhána* Kesavabhatta, who in Saka 1108 was governing the Belvola country; and the *Mahámandalesvara* Kámadeva, of the family of the Kádambas of Banawási and Hángal, who in Saka 1111 was governing the Banavase Twelve-thousand, the Pánungal Five-hundred, and the Puligere Three-hundred. The last of his inscriptions is dated Saka 1111 (A.D. 1189-90), the Saumya *samvatsara*. What became of Somesvara IV. after that date, is not yet known; but the power of the Western Chálukyas, as a dynasty, may be considered to have been then finally extinguished.

There are a few later inscriptions,—such as a grant of Kámvadevaráya of Kalyána, dated Saka 1182 (A.D. 1260-1);[3] an undated grant of Vira-Satyásraya, the son of Govinda, also of Kalyána;[4] and a grant of Vira-Nonamba, also of Kalyána, which falsely assumes to be dated in Saka 366 (A.D. 444-5),[5]—which

---

1 Lat. 14° 25′ N., Long. 75° 30′ E.

2 Elliot *MS. Collection*, Vol. II., pp. 27 to 49, and 126, 233, and 234.

3 *Jour. Bo. Br. R. As. Soc.*, Vol. IV., p. 97; and *Jour. R. As. Soc.*, O.S., Vol. II., p. 388, and Vol. V., p. 177.

4 British Museum Plates; unpublished.

5 *Ind. Ant.*, Vol. VIII., p. 94.

purport to be inscriptions of the descendants of the Western Chálukyas. But, shortly after the date of Saka 1111 mentioned above, the Western Chálukya sovereignty and dominions were apportioned for a time between the Hoysalas of Dvárasamudra from the south and the Yádavas of Devagiri from the north, and were finally possessed in their entirety by the latter.

SECTION VII.

THE KALACHURIS OR KALACHURYAS.

As all the members of this family had the title of *Kálanjara-puravar-ádhisvara*, or 'supreme lord of Kálanjara, the best of cities,' it is plain that the original stock started from that city, which is now represented by the hill-fort of Kálanjar in Bandelkhand. And in the ninth, tenth, and eleventh centuries A.D., a powerful branch of the family was settled near there, and possessed the country of Chedi or Bandelkhand. An account of this branch has been published by General Cunningham.[1] The first historical name is that of Kokalla or Kokkalla I., who is attributed to the end of the ninth century A.D. But, as the inscriptions of this branch of the family are dated in an era, called both the Kalachuri-Samvat and the Chedi-Samvat, the initial date of which has been shown by General Cunningham to lie probably somewhere in A. D. 249,[2] it would seem that the members of it had established their sovereignty long before the time for which we have as yet obtained historical records of them. They call themselves Haihayas, as well as Kalachuris, and claim descent from Yadu through Kártavirya or Sahasrabáhu-Arjuna. And their capital was Tripura, the modern Tewar, a small village about six miles to the west of Jabalpur. We have already noticed some of them in connection with intermarriages between their family and the Ráshtrakutás and Western Chálukyas. Thus,—of the Ráshtrakutas, Krishna II. married a daughter of Kokkalla I.; Jagattunga II. married Lakshmi and Govindámbá, the daughters of Samkaragana I. or Ranavigraha, the son of Kokkalla I.; Indra IV. married Dvijámbá, the great-granddaughter of Kokkalla I.; and Amoghavarsha II. married Kundakadevi, the daughter of Yuvarája, who probably was Yuvarája I. of the Kalachuri family;—and, of the Western Chálukyas, Vikramáditya IV. married Bonthádevi or Vonthádevi, the daughter of Lakshmana, the son of Yuvarája I. Further than this, the Kalachuris of Tripura do not enter into the scope of the present paper.

We have also had indications of some of the Kalachuris having, in earlier times, established themselves more to the south, in the dominions afterwards acquired by the Chalukyas. Thus, in the sixth century A.D., Mangalisa is poetically described as "obtaining as his wife the lovely woman who was the goddess of the fortunes of the Katachchuris," and as "becoming the husband, by ravishment, of the queens of the Kálachchuris." And the Buddharája, son of Samkaragana, whom he drove out, apparently from the Konkanas, very probably was, as General Cunningham has suggested,[3] an early king of the Kalachuri dynasty; this, in fact, seems to be rendered

---

1 *Archæological Reports*, Vol. IX., pp. 54 &c. 2 *Id.*, p. 111. 3 *Id.*, p. 77.

almost certain by the Maháküta column inscription of Mangalisa, which, after mentioning the conquest of king Buddha and the seizure of his riches, records that the wealth of the Kalatsuris,—evidently a Sanskritised form of the name Kalachuri,—was given to the temple of Makutesvara. Also the Haihayas whom Vinayáditya subjugated, and a princess of whose family, Lokamahádevi, was married to his grandson Vikramáditya II., must have been of the same clan with the Kalachuris, even if they did not belong to their particular branch of it.

But we have no connected account of the Kalachuris of the south, until we come to the twelfth century A.D. We then meet with them first as *Mahámandalervaras*, or great feudatory nobles, possessed of the title of 'supreme lord of Kálanjara, the best of cities,' and entitled to carry the banner of a golden bull,[1] and to have the musical instrument called *damaruka*[2] played before them. Their inscriptions point distinctly to their belonging to the same original stock with the Kalachuris of Tripura; but they fail as yet to make it clear whether they were the lineal descendants of the last of the Kalachuris of Tripura, or whether they were descended from a branch of the family which had separated from the original stock and had established itself in the south before the northern Kalachuris established themselves at Tripura. The tradition that they do give as to the origin of the family is that the founder of it, Krishna by name, was the son of a Bráhman girl by the god Siva.[3] Passing himself off as a barber, he contrived to kill, at the city of Kálanjara, an evil-minded king who practised cannibalism.[4] He thus acquired the province of Dahalá, *i.e.* Dáhala or Chedi, and established the Kalachuri family.

The accounts which are given of the descendants of Krishna differ.[5] None of them agree till we come to the names of Jogama, the grandfather, and Permádi, the father, of Bijjala. Starting with Jogama, the genealogy stands as below :—

Jogama.
|
Permádi.
(Saka 1050.)
|
- Bijjala. (Saka 1078 to 1089.)
  - Somesvara. (Saka 1089 to 1097.)
  - Sankama. (Saka 1097 to 1102.)
  - A'havamalla. (Saka 1098 to 1105.)
  - Singhana. (Saka 1105.)
- Siriyádevi, (married to Chávunda II., of the Sindas of Erambarage.)

---

1 *Suvarnavrishabhadhvaja*. 2 A double drum, shaped like an hour-glass.

3 *P. S. and O.-C. Inscriptions*, No. 121.

4 This looks somewhat like an invention to explain the name,—as we have in Kanarese *chura* and *surige*, as corruptions of the Sanskrit *kshura*, *kshuriká*, *chhuriká*, 'a razor, a knife;' and a connection might easily be made between the first two syllables, *kala*, and the Kanarese *kali*, 'to kill.'

5 *P. S. and O.-C. Inscriptions*, No. 121; Elliot *MS. Collection*, Vol. II., p. 148; and *Ind. Ant.*, Vol. IV., p. 274.

Jogama, and Permádi.

Of Jogama, we have no historical details. And of Permádi, all that we know is that in Saka 1050 (A.D. 1128-9), the Kilaka *samvatsara*, he was governing the Taddevádi country, as the feudatory *Mahámandalesvara* of the Western Chálukya king Somesvara III.[1]

Bijjala.

The earliest mention that we have of Bijjala,—also called Bijja, Bijjana, Vijjala, Vijjana, Tribhuvanamalla, and Nissankamalla I.,—shows him to have been the contemporary and feudatory of the Western Chálukya king Jagadekamalla II., in whose time Vijayapándya, of the Pándya family, had the government of the Nonambavádi Thirty-two-thousand, in subordination to Bijjala.[2] We have already seen that Bijjala's first step towards dispossessing the Western Chálukyas of the sovereignty was his being employed as commander-in-chief under Taila III., in one of whose inscriptions, at Bijápur, dated Saka 1073 (A.D. 1151-2), Bijjala is specifically mentioned as the feudatory of Taila, with other officers under him in the government of the Taddevádi Thousand. His own inscriptions are dated as if his reign began in Saka 1078 (A.D. 1156-7), the Dhátu *samvatsara*; and probably he was virtually independent from about that date. But,—as it was not till Saka 1083 (A.D. 1161-2) or 1084, shortly before or shortly after the death of Taila III., that he ceased to call himself a *Mahámandalesvara*, and assumed the regal titles,—he seems to have maintained for some little time longer a show of subordination to the Chálukya king. The exact date of the assumption of the sovereignty by Bijjala cannot yet be fixed. But it is determined, as lying somewhere between the day of the new-moon of the month Pausha of Saka 1083 (A.D. 1161-2), the Vishu *samvatsara*, and the same day in the following year, the Chitrabhánu *samvatsara*, by two inscriptions, of these dates respectively, at Balagámve[3] and Annigeri:[4] in the former of them, Bijjala still styles himself only a *Mahámandalesvara*; while, in the latter of them, he is invested with the usual regal titles of *samastabhuvanásraya*, *prithivivallabha*, *mahárájádhirája* and *paramesvara*, and Annigeri is called the *rájadháni-pattana*, or, 'royal capital.' His inscriptions are found at Balagámve, Tálgund, and Harihar, in Maisur; at Ablur, Rattehalli, Annigeri, and other places, in the Dhárwád District; at Huli in the Belgaum District; at Yekkumbi near Tásgaum; and at Mudgal and Chikka-Muddanur, in the Nizám's Dominions.[5] They show, therefore, that he thoroughly established his power throughout the Chálukya dominions. His principal feudatories and officials were,—the *Dandanáyaka* Barmarasa, who in Saka 1083 (A.D. 1161-2) was governing the Banavase country; the *Dandanáyaka* Sridhara, who in the same year was governing at the capital of Annigeri; and Kásapayyanáyaka, who in Saka 1085 (A.D. 1163-4) was governing the Banavase Twelve-thousand and the Pánungal Five-hundred. The exact year in which he established himself at Kalyána is not apparent; but he did make that city his capital after Annigeri. The latest of his inscriptions is dated in Saka 1089 (A.D. 1167-68), the Sarvajit *samvatsara*, in the

---

1 Elliot *MS. Collection*, Vol. I., p. 687. 2 *P. S. and O.-C. Inscriptions*, No. 120.
3 Elliot *MS. Collection*, Vol. II., p. 67; and *P. S. and O.-C. Inscriptions*, No. 184.
4 Elliot *MS. Collection*, Vol. II., p. 72.
5 Elliot *MS. Collection*, Vol. II., pp. 61 to 121; and *P. S. and O.-C. Inscriptions*, Nos. 101, 119 to 121, 182 to 187, and 219.

twelfth year of his reign. The Kalachuris were Jains. But Bijjala had always shown a considerable amount of favour and liberality to the Saivas; and his death was brought about by the growing power of that sect, or rather of a new division of it, the Lingáyats, founded by the celebrated Basava. This led to a revolution which resulted in the assassination of Bijjala. I take the following account of this revolution, based on the *Basava-Purána*, the text-book of the Lingáyats, and the *Bijjalánkakávya* or *Bijjalacharitra*, the text-book of the Jains, almost *verbatim* from Sir Walter Elliot's paper:[1] —"Basava was born at Bágewádi, in the Bágewádi Táluká of the Kaládgi District, a few miles north of the Krishná, according to local tradition; though the *Purána* ascribes that honour to the neighbouring village of Ingleswar. His father's name was Madhubhatta, or Madigaráya, an A'rádhya or Saiva Bráhman; his mother was named Madalámbiká; and he had a sister named Padmávati, who is described as having been very beautiful. The family seem to have left Bágewádi and gone to Kalyána, where Basava formed an alliance with the chief minister, by marrying his daughter, named Gangámbá; soon after which, Bijjala, having seen the beautiful Padmávati, became enamoured of and married her; and in consequence of these connections her brother was appointed minister and general, in succession, to his brother-in-law. The king gave himself up to the charms of his beautiful bride, and left all power in the hands of Basava, who employed the opportunity thus afforded him to strengthen his own influence, by displacing all the old officers of state and putting in adherents of his own, whilst at the same time he sedulously cultivated the favour of the prince. He likewise began to promulgate a new rule of faith, differing from both that of the Jains and that of the Bráhmans, hitherto the most popular sects. He abolished the distinction of castes, all his followers being enrolled by a particular ceremony into a new and equal order. He himself, and the priests under him, named Jamgamas, were regarded as incarnations of the deity. They observed the same strict abstinence from animal food as the rival sects, and were equally strict and minute in the circumstances to be observed in cooking and eating; but they rejected many of the previously entertained opinions regarding purity and impurity. The great objects of adoration were the *linga*,[2] and Nandi, or the sacred bull that carries Siva, of which Basava proclaimed himself an incarnation.[3] The effigy of their creed, a small stone *linga* in a silver box or shrine, was suspended to the neck, instead of being bound round the arm, according to the practice of the A'rádhyas. It is evident that there is much of the Saiva doctrines, professed by the A'rádhya Bráhmans to which Basava belonged, incorporated in the new creed. Basava increased rapidly in power, and at length roused the fears of Bijjala, who endeavoured to seize his person. He made his escape, however, and fled. Pursuit was ordered; but Basava, collecting some of his followers, attacked and dispersed the party. His adherents flocked to him; and Bijjala, advancing in person to quell

---

1 *Madras Jour. of Lit. and Science*, Vol. VII., pp. 212-4. 2 The phallic emblem.
3 The name of Basava is itself a corruption of the Sanskrit *vrishabha*, 'a bull.'

the insurrection, suffered a complete defeat. He was compelled to submit to his victorious minister, who returned with him to Kalyána, reinstated in all his dignities. Basava, on his return, not only resumed all his former power and authority, but even attempted the life of Bijjala, probably with the intention of governing unmolested during the minority of his nephew, the son of the king and Padmávati, who is named Immadi-Bijjala and Vira-Bijjala. In this he eventually succeeded; but authorities differ as to the manner. The Jain chronicle relates that the king, having marched against the Siláhára, a rebellious feudatory, the *Mahámandalesvara* of Kolhápur, was returning successfully from the expedition, when Basava found means to poison him on the banks of the Bhimá. The *Purána* relates that he was assassinated in the midst of his court by three of Basava's followers, named Jagaddeva, Bommayya, and Mallayya. While a third legend asserts that Madiwála, Máchayya, and Bommayya, the *Masálchis* or torch-bearers of Basava, having concealed their weapons in the roll of cloth serving for a flambeau, stabbed the king whilst preceding their master into his presence. This event is said in the *Bijjalánkakávya* to have occurred in the year 4255 of the Kaliyuga, which corresponds with Saka 1076 (A.D. 1154-5). Bijjala's death, however, according to the inscriptions, did not occur till twelve years later, in Saka 1089 (A. D. 1167-8). It is probable, therefore, that there may be a clerical error in the manuscript. The murder, however perpetrated, did not go unpunished. Basava, dreading the vengeance of the young king, here called the *Yuvarája*, probably the Ráyamurári-Sovideva of the inscriptions, fled to Vrishabhapura, on the Malabar coast. Thither the king pursuing him, laid siege to the city. It was reduced to extremity, and Basava in despair threw himself into a well and was drowned. His body was taken out and ignominiously thrown without the city walls; and thenceforward the name of the city was called Ulavi, because Basava thought he would there save himself, a name which it still retains.[1] The sect, however, found a more able, or at least a more successful, leader in Channabasava, the son of another sister of Basava, named Akka-Nágamma, or according to others Nágalámbiká, by whom the Lingáyat belief was completely established. It is now the prevailing form of worship throughout the whole of the country where the Kanarese language is spoken, comprising the greater portion of the Nizám's Dominions, the Southern Maráthá Country, Sundá, Maisur, Ballári, &c."

Bijjala was succeeded, in Saka 1089 (A.D. 1167-8), the Sarvajit *samvatsara*, by his eldest son Somesvara, also called Sovideva and Ráyamurári. His inscriptions are found at Balagámve, A'nawatti, and Tálgund in Maisur; at Annigeri, Rattehalli, Lakkundi, Narsápur, and other places, in the Dhárwád District; at Ingleswar in the Kaládgi Somesvara.

1 Ulavi, the 'Woolwi' of maps, is about fourteen miles to the west of Yellápur in the North Kanara District, at the foot of the Ghauts; it is a celebrated place of Lingáyat pilgrimage.—The above account of Basava's death is taken entirely from the Jain chronicle. The Lingáyats maintain that he was absorbed into the *linga* at the temple of Samgamesvara at Kapila-Samgam, which is at the junction of the Krishná and the Malaprabhá rivers in the Kaládgi District; and a depression in the surface of the *linga* is still shown as the spot at which he entered it.

District; and at Kukkanur and other places in the Nizám's Dominions.[1] His principal feudatories and officials were,—the *Dandanáyaka* Kesava or Kesimayya, who in Saka 1090 (A.D. 1168-9) was governing the Taddevádi Thousand, the Pánungal Five-hundred, and the Banavase Twelve-thousand; the *Dandanáyaka* Tejimayya, who was the governor of the Belvola country, and who in Saka 1092 (A.D. 1170-1) conquered the Kukkanur *Ágrahára*; the *Mahápradhána* and *Senápati* Mádhavayyanáyaka; and the *Mahámandalesvara* Vijayapándya, evidently a second of the same name, of the Pándya family, who in Saka 1096 (A.D. 1174-5) was governing the Banavase country. His capital was Kalyána; but he seems also to have had a seat of government at Modeganur. His reign was apparently an uneventful one, none of his inscriptions recording any wars or conquests of any great importance.

Sankama, A'havamalla, and Singhana.

Somesvara was succeeded, either late in Saka 1097 (A.D. 1175-6), the Manmatha *samvatsara*, or early in Saka 1098, the Durmukha *samvatsara*, by his younger brother Sankama, also called Nissankamalla II. But the synchronous dates of their inscriptions show that his brothers A'havamalla and Singhana were associated with him in the government. And the localities in which the inscriptions of the three brothers are found show that, even before Somesvara IV. in Saka 1104 (A.D. 1882-3) re-established the Western Chálukya sovereignty for a short while in the southern parts of the Chálukya dominions, the power of Sankama, A'havamalla, and Singhana, in that part of the country, must have been of a very limited and partial kind, and probably had already begun to be disputed by Somesvara IV. The inscriptions of Sankama are found at Kaulur and Kukkanur, and a few other places, in the Nizám's Dominions; at Ron, Sudi, and a few other places, in the Dhárwád District; and at Balagámve, Harihar, and Halebid, in Maisur; and they range from Saka 1099 (A.D. 1177-8) to Saka 1102 (A.D. 1180-1).[2] His capital was Kalyána; but Modeganur also was one of his seats of government. His principal feudatories and officials were,—the *Mahápradhána* and *Dandanáyaka* Kesirája, who in Saka 1101 (A.D. 1179-80) was governing the Banavase country, with a certain Sampakara, of the Gutta family, apparently in subordination to him; and Vikrama, of the Sinda family, who in Saka 1102 was governing the Kisukád Seventy. This Vikrama was a cousin, by marriage, of Sankama, being the son of Chávunda II. by his second wife Siriyádevi, who was the sister of Bijjala. The inscriptions of A'havamalla are found at Hodal and Chikka-Muddanur in the Nizám's Dominions; at Aniveri in the Dhárwád District; and at Balagámve and Halebid in Maisur;[3] and they range from Saka 1102 to Saka 1105, which was the eighth year of his reign. One of them mentions, as his feudatory, Vikramáditya of the Gutta or Gupta family, or lineage of Chandragupta. The only inscription of Singhana known to me is a copper-plate grant found at Behatti in the

---

1 Elliot *MS. Collection*, Vol. II., pp. 133 to 189; and *P. S. and O.-C. Inscriptions*, Nos. 101, 183, 185, 188, and 220.

2 Elliot *MS. Collection*, Vol. II., pp. 57, 58, and 199 to 257; and *P. S. and O.-C. Inscriptions*, Nos. 122, 183, 189 to 193, and 230.

3 Elliot *MS. Collection*, Vol. II., pp. 229 to 251; and *P. S. and O.-C. Inscriptions*, Nos. 190 to 193, and 230.

Dhárwád District; it is dated Saka 1105 (A.D. 1183-4), and records a grant of the village of Kukkanur in the Belvola Three-hundred.[1] One of A'havamalla's inscriptions speaks of wars between him and the Cholas, the Hoysalas, and a Vijayáditya, who seems to have been the second of that name of the family of the Kádambas of Goa.[2] But, with this exception, the inscriptions of these three brothers do not give us much insight into the history of the period and the events that led to the downfall of the Kalachuris. This must have occurred in, or soon after, Saka 1105 (A.D. 1183-4), as nothing is known of the family after that date; and it was effected by the Hoysalas, under Ballála II. or Vira-Ballála,[3] who shortly after acquired the sovereignty over the whole of the country of Kuntala.

---

1 *Ind. Ant.*, Vol. IV., p. 274.
2 *P. S. and O.-C. Inscriptions*, No. 192.
3 *Ind. Ant.*, Vol. II., p. 302.

SECTION VIII.

THE HOYSALAS.—

The Kalachuris were succeeded by the Hoysalas, Hoysanas, Poysalas, or Poysanas. And,—as one of Sankama's inscriptions[1] records a grant of the village of Kaurur or Kaulur, in the Másavádi country, by the *Mahámandalesvara* Vira-Ballála or Ballála II.; and also as the regal titles were first assumed by Ballála II., the title of *Mahámandalesvara* only being borne by himself in his early years, and by his ancestors,—it seems probable that, just before they obtained the supreme sovereignty, the Hoysalas were feudatories of the Kalachuris, as the Kalachuris had been of the Western Chálukyas before them.

The following is the Hoysala genealogy, as established by the inscriptions, and commencing with Vinayáditya, who is the first historical person in the family, though the original founder of it is said to have been one Sala:—

Vinayáditya.
(Saka 969 and 998.)

Ereyanga.

Ballála I. (Saka 1025.) | Vishnuvardhana. (Saka 1039 and 1059.) | Udayáditya

Narasimha I.

Ballála II.,
or Vira-Ballála.
(Saka 1113 and 1133.)

Narasimha II.
(Saka 1145.)

Somesvara.
(Saka 1174.)

Narasimha III.
(Saka 1176 and 1208.)

Ballála III.
(Saka 1232.)

---

1 Elliot *MS. Collection*, Vol. II., p. 199.

The Hoysalas belonged to the lineage of Yadu; and hence *Yádava-Náráyana* was one of their family-titles, as it was also of the Yádavas of Devagiri. And the tradition as to the derivation of their dynastic name is that an early member of the family, Sala by name, living at the city of Sasakapura, preserved the life of an ascetic at that city, by destroying a tiger that had come to devour him while engaged in the performance of his religious duties. The words used by the ascetic, in calling for succour, were *Poy Sala* or *Hoy Sala*, *i.e.* "Slay, O Sala!" By this achievement Sala, and after him his descendants, acquired the name of Poysala or Hoysala, and became entitled to carry the device of a tiger on their banners.[1]

When, however, the family first becomes historically known, the Hoysalas were settled at Dvárávatipura, Dvárasamudra, or Dhorasamudra, the modern Halebid in Maisur.[2] From this they derived another family title, which also was shared by the Yádavas of Devagiri,—that of *Dvárávati-puravar-ádhisvara*, or 'supreme lord of Dvárávati, the best of cities.' They were *Mahámandalesvaras*, entitled, as has been said, to carry the banner of a tiger.[3] And their family-goddess was Vásantikádevi of Sasakapura.

Vinayáditya.

Vinayáditya, whose wife was Keleyabbe, is the first of the family of whom we have any authentic mention. The number of generations that had intervened between him and Sala is nowhere recorded; and, as none of the inscriptions mention his immediate ancestors, he seems to have been the first of the family to enjoy any substantial power. Of his own time there is only one inscription,—the first part of a stone-tablet at Sindigere in Maisur,[4] the latter part of which belongs to the time of his grandson Vishnuvardhana. It gives him the title of Tribhuvanamalla I., and speaks of him as a *Mahámandalesvara*, subordinate to the Western Chálukya king Vikramáditya VI.; and it records that in Saka 961[5] he was, or had been, governing all the country included between the Konkana, the country of Bhadadavayal, Talakád, and Sávimale. And an inscription at Nirgund in Maisur,[6]—the preamble of which must refer to him, though, in addition to Tribhuvanamalla, it calls him Víraganga, which title in the later inscriptions is given only to his grandsons Ballála and Vishnuvardhana,—makes him a contemporary of the Ganga king Kongalivarmá, and records that in Saka 987[7] he was ruling the Gangavádi Ninety-six-thousand. The inscriptions of his descendants also state that he conquered the Konkana; but it is not probable that this conquest extended anywhere north of the present district of North Kanara, as the Kádambas of Goa were sufficiently powerful to hold him in check in that direction, in addition to their being at that time on friendly terms with Vikramáditya VI., who was the Chálukya viceroy at Banawási, and of whom Vinayáditya himself was, as has been stated, a feudatory.

---

[1] *Ind. Ant.*, Vol. II., p. 301.

[2] Lat. 13° 12′ N., Long. 76° 2′ E.

[3] *Sárduladhvaja.*

[4] *Mysore Inscriptions*, p. 320.

[5] As, however, the inscription specifies the name of the *samvatsara* as Sarvajit, Saka 961 must be a mistake for Saka 969 (A.D. 1047-8). Even this, however, seems too early a date for the viceroyship of Vikramáditya VI.

[6] *Mysore Inscriptions*, p. 307.

[7] Here, again, as the inscription specifies the name of the *samvatsara* as Nala, Saka 987 must be a mistake for Saka 998 (A.D. 1076-7).

Ereyanga. Of the time of his son, Ereyanga, there are no inscriptions. In one of the later inscriptions, in which his name is written both Ereyanga and Ereganga, he is said to have made conquests in the north, and to have subjugated the territories that had been held by Bhoja of Dhárá, the king of Málava. His wife was Echaladevi.

Ballála I. Of his eldest son, Ballála I., the only record that we have is that he overcame Jagaddeva, the Sántara king of Patti-Pombuchchapura, whom we have already mentioned in connection with the Western Chálukya king Jagadekamalla II.;—and that in Saka 1025 (A.D. 1103-4), the Svabhánu *samvatsara*, while governing at his capital of Belápura, the modern Belur [1] in Maisur, he married Padmaladevi, Chávalidevi, and Boppadevi, the three daughters of the *Dandanáyaka* Mariyáne, who had been invested by Vinayáditya with the lordship of Sindigere.

Vishnuvardhana. Of the time of Vishnuvardhana,—also called Bitti, Bittiga, Tribhuvanamalla II., Bhujabalaganga, Viraganga, and Vikramaganga, —we have only three inscriptions;[3] two of them are dated Saka 1039 (A.D. 1117-8), the Hemalambi *samvatsara*, and Saka 1060 for 1059 (A.D. 1137-8), the Pingala *samvatsara*; the date of the third is not known. His wife was Sántaladevi, also called Lakumádevi in one of the inscriptions. The inscriptions of himself and of his successors give many details concerning him, and show that it was he who first established the independence of the Hoysalas, though he did not assume any higher title than that of *Mahámandalesvara*. The earliest facts that we have in connection with him are that he fixed the boundaries of the Hoysala kingdom, and that he took and burnt Talakád or Talavanapura, the capital of the Gangas, and established himself in their dominions; it was by this achievement that he acquired the titles of Bhujabalaganga, Viraganga, and Vikramaganga. One of the passages descriptive of him in the later inscriptions states that, when he set out on his campaign, "Kánchi fled before him; Kongu was shaken to its foundations; the excellent Virátakote (or Hángal) cried out; Koyatur (which is probably a shorter form of Koyimmuttur or Coimbatore) was dishevelled and destroyed; the famous Chakragotta (or the Chakrakota of which we have had mention in connection with the Western Chálukya king Vikramáditya VI.) made way for him; and the seven Konkanas threw down their arms and took refuge in the ocean."[4] He is also said to have been victorious against the Pándya and Tulu kings,—to have broken the power of Jagaddeva of Patti-Pombuchchapura,—to have subdued the Kádambas of Goa under Jayakesi II.,—to have conquered the Vengiri king and Narasimha, to have taken Uchchangi,—and to have become the lord of the Male kings. He also acquired the Kongu country, Nonambavádi, Kolálapura, Kovatur, Tereyur, Vallur, and Kánchi. His seat of government was at Belápura; and his power is said to have extended over Talakád, Kongu, Nangali, Gangavádi, Nolambavádi or Nonambavádi, Másavádi, Huligere, Halasige, Banavase, and Pánungal. The

---

1 Lat. 13° 10′ N., Long. 75° 55′ E. 2 *Mysore Inscriptions*, p. 330.
3 *P. S. and O.-C. Inscriptions*, Nos. 18 and 232; and the Sindigere inscription quoted above.
4 *P. S. and O.-C. Inscriptions*, No. 123, l. 24.

Halasige district was acquired by the conquest of Jayakesi II. of the family of the Kádambas of Goa, and the Banavâse and Pánungal districts by the conquest of Tailapa II. of the family of the Kádambas of Banawási and Hángal. Vishnuvardhana, however, does not seem to have retained any of the Kádamba districts for any length of time. It was probably in his time that the Konkana was conquered, and tribute was levied from Vijayáditya II., of the family of the Kádambas of Goa, by some unspecified chieftains who were afterwards the feudatories of Ballála II.[1] The boundaries of his kingdom are specifically defined in one of his inscriptions, and are said to be Sávimale on the north, the lower Nangali Ghaut on the east, the Kongu, Chera, and Anamale countries on the south, and the Bárakanur Ghaut road to the Konkana on the west. In one of the later inscriptions he is said to have invaded the Belvola country up to the Krishnaverná,[2] and to have ingratiated himself with Permádi or Vikramáditya VI. But this would seem to be an exaggeration; as, though he undoubtedly did invade the Chálukya dominions, yet the Sinda inscriptions tell us that he was repulsed, on behalf of the Chálukyas, by A'chugi II., and again by Permádi I., who pursued him into his own territories, besieged Dhorasamudra, and captured the city of Belupura.[3] One of these Sinda inscriptions enumerates, as the dominions of Vishnuvardhana, the countries of Bengiri or Vengiri, Chera, Chola, Malaya, Maleyel, Tulu, Kolla, and Pallava, the city of Konguna, and the countries of Banavâse, Kadambale, and Hayve.

The inscriptions give no account of Udayáditya beyond the mention of his name; and it seems unlikely, therefore, that he ever had any part in the government of the Hoysala kingdom. Udayáditya.

The successor of Vishnuvardhana was, therefore, his son, Narasimha I., whose wife was Echaladevi. No historical details are mentioned in connection with him except that the Nirgund inscription, speaking of 'his standards reaching as far as the peaks of Devagiri.' would seem to imply that he made an expedition in that direction; this, however, requires to be verified. Narasimha I.

He was succeeded by his son Ballála II.,—usually called Vira-Ballála, but also known by the name of Giridurgamalla, or 'the conqueror of hill-forts,'—whose wife was Padmaladevi. His inscriptions are found at Belur, Halebid, Sorab, Tálgund, Harihar, and Balagámve, in Maisur; and at Balaganur, Benkankond, Sátenhalli, Alawandi, Hángal, Mulgund, Mewundi, Annigeri, Nágámve, and Gadag, in the Dhárwád District.[4] They range from Saka 1114 (A.D. 1192-3) to Saka 1133 (A.D. 1211-2), the Prajotpatti *samvatsara*; Ballála II.

---

1 *P. S. and O.-C. Inscriptions*, No. 192.

2 *i. e.* the Krishná. It is usually, if not always, called the Krishnaverná in inscriptions. The passage which shows that the two names are identical is in an inscription, of the time of the Devagiri-Yádava king Singhana II., at Mankani, in the Bágalkot Táluká of the Kaládgi District, which is on the south bank of the Krishná; it records the building and endowment of the temple of Bhásuradeva at Mankani on the banks of the Krishnaverná.

3 It is probably only by a metrical license that, in the passage in question, this form is used for the Belápura of the other inscriptions.

4 Elliot *MS. Collection*, Vol. II., pp. 265 to 334; and *P. S. and O.-C. Inscriptions*, Nos. 18, 98, 99, 106, 194 to 200, 221, 223, 224, and 233.

and they fix Saka 1113 (A.D. 1191-2), the Virodhikrit *samvatsara*, for the commencement of his reign. It was he who first of his family assumed the regal titles, and, by defeating Brahmá or Barma, the general of the Kalachuri army, established the power of the Hoysalas north of the Tungabhadrá in the Kalachuri dominions; but this must have been some seven or eight years before the commencement of his own reign, and while he was serving as the commander-in-chief of his father's forces. He seems, however, never to have penetrated permanently north of the Malápahári or Malaprabhá river. In Saka 1114, we find him established at the capital of Lokkigundi, the modern Lakkundi[1] near Gadag in the Dhárwád District. And before that time, in addition to defeating the Kalachuris, he had met and defeated Jaitrasimha or Jaitugi I., the son of Bhillama of the Yádava dynasty of Devagiri, by which victory he acquired the supremacy over the country of Kuntala; this battle between Ballála and Jaitrasimha is said by tradition to have been fought at Lakkundi itself.[2] An inscription of his son, Narasimha II., also gives a graphic account of a battle between him and a certain Semana or Sevuna, whom he besieged and defeated at Soratur near Gadag, and pursued from there up to the Krishnaverná, where he slew him, and who was probably the commander-in-chief of Jaitugi's army. In the same campaign Ballála besieged, besides Soratur, the hill-forts of Erambarage or Yelburga, Virátakote or Hángal, Gutti, Bellittage, Rattapalli or Rattehalli in the Dhárwád District, and Kurugod near Ballári.[3] His conquests also included the Chola and Pándya kings, to the latter of whom he restored his forfeited kingdom when he humbled himself before him,—Uchchangi,—part of the Konkana,—and the districts of Banavàse and Pánungal. His first attempt on the last district was made in Saka 1118 (A.D. 1196-7), when he besieged Pánungal which was then the capital of the *Mahámandalesvara* Kámadeva, of the family of the Kádambas of Banawási and Hángal, who was governing the Pánungal Five-hundred. In this attempt he was unsuccessful, being repulsed by Kámadeva's generals Sohani and his son Padmayya or Padmana, the former of whom was killed in the battle. In addition to Lokkigundi, he had also a capital at Annigeri in the Dhárwád District. In Saka 1114 (A.D. 1192-3), we find his *Mahápradhána* and *Dandanáyaka*, Ereyana or Eraga, governing the Banavase Twelve-thousand and the Sántalige Thousand; in Saka 1121 (A.D. 1199-1200) his feudatory, the *Mahámandalesvara* Ráyadeva, was governing the Belvola country; in Saka 1124 (A.D. 1202-3) his feudatory, the *Mahámandalesvara* Jagadala-Bhattamadeva, was governing the Kuntala country; and in Saka 1125 his *Dandanáyaka*, Kamathada-Mallisetti, was governing the Sántalige Seventy and the Nágarakhanda Seventy in the Banavase country.

Narasimha II. He was succeeded by his son, Narasimha II., who lost entirely, through the increasing power of the Yádavas of Devagiri, the

1 Lat. 15° 24′ N., Long. 75° 47′ E.
2 Sir Walter Elliot; *Madras Jour. of Lit. and Science*, Vol. VII., p. 216.
3 *P. S. and O.-C. Inscriptions*, No. 123, l. 33.

kingdom that his father had acquired in the old Western Chálukya dominions. He retired to his capital of Dvárasamudra, and seems to have made no attempt to come north of the Tungabhadrá again. Only one inscription of his time has been discovered,—at Harihar in Maisur, dated Saka 1145 (A.D. 1233-4) the Svabhánu *samvatsara*.[1] He is said to have dispossessed the Pándya king of his dominions, and to have given them to the Chola king. But his reign seems to have been a quiet one; and the chief event in it was the building of the temple of the god Harihara at Harihar by his *Mahápradhána* and *Dandanáyaka* Polálva.

Somesvara.

His successor was his son Somesvara, of whose time we have two inscriptions,—a stone-tablet at Nirgund in Maisur; and a copper-plate grant now in the Bangalore Museum, but where found originally I do not know.[2] The latter is dated Saka 1175 for 1174 (A.D. 1242-3), the Paridhávi *samvatsara*; the former is not dated. His wives were Bijjaladevi and Somaladevi. And his capital was Vikramapura, "which he had established for his own pleasure in the Chola country, conquered by the power of his arm."

Narasimha III.

His successor was his son Narasimha III., by his wife Bijjaladevi. Of his time we have six inscriptions,—at Belur, Chitaldurg, Harihar, and Somnáthpur, in Maisur;[3] the earliest of them is dated Saka 1176 (A.D. 1254-5), the A'nanda *samvatsara*, and the latest, Saka 1208 (A.D. 1286-7), the Vyaya *samvatsara*. His capital was Dvárasamudra. All the history that we have in connection with him is that his *Mahápradhána* and *Dandanáyaka* Perumáledeva, also called Ráüttaráya and Javanike-Náráyana, conquered and slew a certain king named Ratnapála.

Ballála III.

Of the time of his son and successor, Ballála III., we have only one inscription,—at Chitaldurg;[4] the figures of the date are effaced, but, as the name of the *samvatsara* is specified as Sádhárana, the date must be Saka 1232 (A.D. 1310-1). The inscription, however, tells us nothing about the history of his reign. And the year in which it is dated saw practically both the end of his reign and the extinction of the power of his dynasty. As will be seen in the following section, Allá-ud-din, the second of the Khilji emperors of Delhi, had already invaded the Dekkan, and had commenced and almost completed the conquest of the Yádavas of Devagiri. As yet, the Hoysalas had remained unattacked. But in A.D. 1310, Allá-ud-din sent an army under Malik Káfur and Khwájá Háji to reduce Dvárasamudra. Leaving part of their forces at Paithán on the Godávari, to overawe and hold in check Samkara of Devagiri, —Malik Káfur and Khwájá Háji continued their march to the south, entered and laid waste the Hoysala kingdom, engaged, defeated, and captured Ballála III., and took and despoiled his capital of Dvárasamudra.[5] The complete subjugation of the province of Dvárasamudra, and the annexation of it to the empire of Delhi,

---

1 Elliot *MS. Collection*, Vol. II., p. 336; and *P. S. and O.-C. Inscriptions*, No. 123.
2 *Mysore Inscriptions*, pp. 307 and 321.
3 *P. S. and O.-C. Inscriptions*, Nos. 18, 19, 20, 124, and 148; and *Mysore Inscriptions*, p. 323.
4 *P. S. and O.-C. Inscriptions*, No. 147.
5 *Ferishta* (Briggs' Translation), Vol. I., p. 373; and Elphinstone's *History of India*, Cowell's edition, p. 396.

were not effected till A.D. 1327, in the reign of Muhammad Tughlak.[1] Meanwhile, though the Muhammadan chronicle does not record the fate of Ballála III., it would appear that, after his defeat and capture in A.D. 1310, he was liberated, and continued for a short time longer the semblance of a reign at the former capital of Belápura; and that, after the events of A.D. 1327, in which Dvárasamudra was demolished, the then representative of the family retired to Tondanur, the modern Tonnur near Seringapatam, which continued to be the seat of an enfeebled power for about fifty years more.[2] The power of the Hoysalas as a dynasty, however, was practically extinguished by the conquest of A.D. 1310.

---

1 *Ferishta*, Vol. I., p. 413.

2 *Mysore Inscriptions*, p. lxxix; and Rice's *Gazetteer of Mysore and Coorg*, Vol. II., p. 297. Ferishta (Vol. I., p. 418-9) tells us that, in A.D. 1338, Báhá-ud-din, more commonly known by his original name of 'Koorshasip,' rebelled against his uncle, Muhammad Tughlak, and, being defeated, deserted his government of Ságar and fled to the Hoysala court; and that he was given up to the king by the then representative of the family, whom Ferishta calls Ballaladeva.

SECTION IX.

THE YA'DAVAS OF DEVAGIRI.

On the downfall of the Kalachuris, the southern parts of their dominions fell, as we have seen, into the hands of the Hoysalas of Dvárasamudra. And, at the same time, the northern parts were appropriated by another branch of the Yádava family, the members of which,—since, like the Hoysalas, they had the family-titles of *Yádava-Náráyana* and *Dvárávati-puravar-ádhisvara*,—must have been of the same original stock with the Hoysalas, though, for some reason or other, the connection between the two families is nowhere acknowledged in the inscriptions. These Yádavas eventually settled themselves at Devagiri, the modern Daulatábád[1] near Aurangábád. Their banner bore the device of a golden Garuda.[2]

The following is the complete genealogy of this dynasty :—

Singhana I.
|
Mallugi.
|
Bhillama.
(Saka 1109 to 1113.)
|
Jaitugi I.
(Saka 1113 to 1131.)
|
Singhana II.
(Saka 1131 to 1169.)
|
Jaitugi II.

- Krishna. (Saka 1169 to 1182.)
  - Rámachandra. (Saka 1193 to 1230.)
    - Samkara. (Saka 1231 to 1233.)
    - Bhima.
    - A daughter, (married to Harapála)
- Mahádeva. (Saka 1182 to 1193.)
  - Amana.

Singhana I., and Mallugi.

The names of Singhana I. and Mallugi are supplied by a recently discovered copper-plate grant of Rámachandra, which seems to have been found somewhere in the neighbourhood of the Godávari in the Aurangábád District.[3] It is recorded therein of Singhana I, that

---

[1] Lat. 19° 57′ N., Long. 75° 25′ E.
[2] *Suvarnagarudadhvaja* ; *Jour. Bo. Br. R. As. Soc.*, Vol. XII., p. 35.
[3] Unpublished.

he subdued the king of the Karnátaka,[1] and punished the Pándya king, and that the king of Gurjara avoided meeting him in battle. Of his son Mallugi, no details are given.

Bhillama.

Mallugi's son was Bhillama, beyond whom none of the other inscriptions as yet known carry back the genealogy. We have already had mention of him in connection with the Hoysala king Ballála II., by whom, apparently in Bhillama's life-time, his son Jaitugi I. was defeated in a battle fought, according to tradition, at Lakkundi in the Dhárwád District. As Ballála is said to have by this victory acquired the country of Kuntala, the prior acquisition of which by Bhillama himself is recorded in his own inscriptions and in those of his descendants, Bhillama must have already established a fairly extensive kingdom. Of his time we have four inscriptions.[2] The earliest of them is at the *Jághir* village of Muttigi; it gives him the usual regal titles, and is dated Saka 1111 (A.D. 1189-90), the third year of his reign, while he was ruling at Tenevalage, with the *Mándalika* Sopani as his *Mahápradhána* and *Senápati.* This inscription, therefore, fixes Saka 1109 (A.D. 1187-8), the Plavamga *samvatsara* for the commencement of his reign. In this inscription he is also called *Málava-malla,* or 'the champion against the Málavas,' and *Gurjara-váran-ánkusa,* or 'the goad to the elephants which are the Gurjaras.' Another, of the same date, is at Annigeri in the Dhárwád District, and speaks of that place as the capital, from which his feudatory, the *Mahámandalesvara* Báchirája or Báchana, was governing the Belvola country. Another, at Bhairwádige in the Kaládgi District, is dated Saka 1113 (A.D. 1191-2). And the last, at Hippargi in the Kaládgi District, is dated Saka 1114 (A.D. 1192-3), while the *Mahámandalesvara* Gonamarasa, who had been his feudatory, was governing the Taddevádi country.

Jaitugi I.

Bhillama was succeeded, in Saka 1113 (A.D. 1191-2), the Virodhikrit *samvatsara,* by his son Jaitugi I., also called Jaitrasimha and Jaitrapála, who had held the supreme command of his father's army when it was defeated by Ballála II. Of his time there are three inscriptions,—at Bijápur, Mannugulli, and the *Jághir* village of Rámoji and Akkoja, in the Kaládgi District.[3] The first of them only is dated,—in Saka 1118 (A.D. 1196-7), the sixth year of his reign. We have no further historical details about him, except that the Aurangábád grant of his descendant Rámachandra states that he slew the king of Trikalinga and took his whole kingdom. Vijayápura, or Bijápur,[4] seems to have been his capital.

Singhana II.

He was succeeded, in Saka 1131 (A.D. 1209-10), the Sukla *samvatsara,* by his son Singhana II., also called Simha, Simhala, Simhana, and Tribhuvanamalla. It is in his time, in Saka 1132, that we first have Devagiri mentioned as the capital. In the early years of his reign we find him using, in addition to the titles of his ancestors, those of 'the uprooter of the water-lily which was the head of the king of Telunga,' and 'the conqueror of the Kalachuri king.' And in the Aurangábád grant he is said to have conquered

---

1 This must refer to some success against the Hoysala king, Vishnuvardhana.
2 Elliot *MS. Collection,* Vol. II., pp. 353 to 362.
3 *Id.,* Vol. II., pp. 369 to 373.
4 Lat. 16° 50′ N., Long. 75° 47′ E.

Ballála, Hammira, Kakkala, the Andhra king, the lord of Bhambhágiri, Bhoja, and Arjuna. Some of these statements remain to be verified; but the Bhoja who is mentioned here is Bhoja II., of the family of the Siláhára *Mahámandalesvaras* of Kolhápur, by the conquest of whom Singhana II., in the early part of his reign, acquired and annexed to his own kingdom the whole of the Siláhára territories above the Ghauts. We have thirty-eight inscriptions of his time,—at Ingalige, Gobbur, and Hagaritige, in the Nizám's Dominions; at Bijápur and a few other places in the Kaládgi District; at Khedrápur in the Kolhápur State; at Munawalli in the Belgaum District; at Gadag, Chaudadámpur, Lakshmeswar, Rattehalli, Tiliwalli, and other places, in the Dhárwád District; and at Balagámve, A'nivatti, and Yalawál, in Maisur.[1] In Saka 1137 (A.D. 1215-6) his *Mahápradhána* Hemmayyanáyaka was the manager of the customs duties of the Banavase country; in Saka 1141 (A.D. 1219-20) Singhana had the whole of the Banavase Twelve-thousand under him; in Saka 1145 (A.D. 1223-4) his *Dandanáyaka* Jagadala-Purushottama was governing the Toragale or Toragal Six-thousand; in Saka 1162 (A.D. 1240-1) his *Mahápradhána* Jaitrapála was governing the Hagaritige Three-hundred; in Saka 1163 (A.D. 1241-2) his *Mahápradhána* Lakshmipála was governing the Nágarakhanda country; and in Saka 1169 (A.D. 1247-8) his *Mahápradhána* and *Senápati* Báchirája was governing the Karnátaka and other countries, at the capital of Pulikaranagara or Lakshmeswar.

Jaitugi II.

His son, Jaitugi II., must have died in Singhana's life-time. He certainly did not reign, as Singhana II. was succeeded immediately by his grandson Krishna; and we have no inscriptions of Jaitugi II., and no record of him beyond the mention of his name.

Krishna.

Of the time of Krishna,—also called Kanhara, Kanhára, Kandhara, and Kandhára,—we have six inscriptions,—at Chikka-Bágewádi and Munawalli in the Belgaum District; and at Gadag, Nágámve, Behatti, and Chaudadámpur, in the Dhárwád District.[2] His accession was in Saka 1169 (A. D. 1247-8), the Plavamga *samvatsara*; and his capital was Devagiri. In Saka 1171 (A.D. 1249-50) his minister was Mallisetti, who governed the Kuhundi or Kundi country from his residence at Mudugal. And in Saka 1175 (A.D. 1253-4) his *Mahápradhána*, in charge of the southern portions of his kingdom, was Chaundarája,—the son of the general Vichana, who had previously acquired for his sovereign the territories of "the Rattas, the Kádambas who were glorious in the Konkana, the Pándyas who shone at Gutti, and the turbulent Hoysalas, and had set up his pillars of victory in the neighbourhood of the river Káveri." And the inscription that mentions Chaundarája records a grant which, with his sovereign's permission, he made at Kukkanur, where he had arrived in the course of a victorious campaign.

Mahádeva.

Krishna was succeeded in the first instance by his younger brother, Mahádeva, called Uragasárvabhauma in the Aurangábád grant,

[1] Elliot *MS. Collection*, Vol. II., pp. 369, and 377 to 459; *P. S. and O.-C. Inscriptions*, Nos. 87, 91, 100, 111, 112, and 201; and *Jour. Bo. Br. R. As. Soc.*, Vol. XII., pp. 7 and 11.

[2] *Jour. Bo. Br. R. As. Soc.*, Vol. XII., pp. 25 and 34; Elliot *MS. Collection*, Vol. II., pp. 467 to 473; and *P. S. and O.-C. Inscriptions*, Nos. 21 and 110.

which contains an expression intimating that he forcibly usurped the sovereignty. We have fourteen inscriptions of his time,—at Kuligeri and Yáligi in the Nizám's Dominions; at Ingleswar in the Kaládgi District; and at Chaudadámpur, Sangur, Pura in the Kod Táluká, and other places, in the Dhárwád District.[1] They range from Saka 1184 (A.D. 1262-3) to Saka 1192 (A.D. 1270-1), and fix Saka 1182 (A.D. 1260-1), the Raudri *samvatsara*, for the commencement of his reign. They do not give many historical details. But in Saka 1184 (A.D. 1262-3) and Saka 1186 we find, as his feudatory in the neighbourhood of Chaudadámpur, the *Mahámandalesvara* Guttarasa of the Gutta or Gupta lineage; in Saka 1187 his *Mahápradhána* was Toragaledevarasa, who made a grant at Vijayápura; and in Saka 1191 (A.D. 1269-70) his *Mahápradhána* and *Sarvádhikári* or 'general manager' was Tipparasa. His capital, throughout his reign, was Devagiri.

Amana.

Mahádeva's son, Amana, is mentioned only in the Aurangábád grant. He seems to have made an attempt to succeed his father, but to have failed, as the inscription describes Rámachandra as forcibly wresting the kingdom from him.

Rámachandra, Samkara, and Bhima.

The succession accordingly went back to Rámachandra or Rámadeva, the son of Krishna, in Saka 1193 (A.D. 1271-2), the Prajápati *samvatsara*. Under him also Devagiri continued to be the capital. Of his time we have, in addition to the Aurangábád grant, nineteen inscriptions,—at Thána in the Konkan; at Neregal in the Hángal Táluká, Lakshmeswar, Chaudadámpur, Rattehalli, and other places, in the Dhárwád District; and at Balagámve, Harihar, and Dávangere, in Maisur.[2] In Saka 1194 (A.D. 1272-3), his *Mahápradhána* Achyutanáyaka was governing the Sásati, or Salsette, district in the Konkana. In Saka 1199 (A.D. 1277-8), his feudatory was the *Mahámandalesvara* Sáluva-Tikkama, who had come to Harihar in the course of a victorious expedition to the south, which had probably been directed against the Hoysalas of Dvárasamudra in consequence of their threatening, or perhaps invading, the southern and south-western parts of his dominions; as, in this inscription, Rámachandra is described as seizing the goddess of the sovereignty of the Hoysala kings, and Sáluva-Tikkama is called 'the establisher of the Kádamba kings' and 'the overthrower of the Hoysala kings.' In Saka 1211 (A.D. 1289-90), in one of the Thána grants, Rámachandra is described as reigning over the whole country of the Konkanas. In Saka 1217 (A.D. 1295-6), his *Mahápradhána* Mallideva was governing the Pulikara or Puligere Three-hundred. And Rámachandra is mentioned as emperor in the concluding lines of a manuscript of the *Námalingánusásana* which was written in Kaliyuga 4398 (A.D. 1297-8) at Suvarnagiri in the Konkana.[3] It is therefore clear that Rámachandra's sway extended over all the dominions, in the central and southern parts of the Bombay Presidency, of the dynasties that had preceded his.

1 Elliot *MS. Collection*, Vol. II., pp. 477 to 507; and *P. S. and O.-C. Inscriptions*, Nos. 110 and 111.

2 Elliot *MS. Collection*, Vol. II., pp. 513 to 530; *P. S. and O.-C. Inscriptions*, Nos 125, 142, and 202 to 205; and *Jour R. As. Soc.*, O. S., Vol. II., p. 388; and Vol. V., pp. 178 and 183.

3 *Ind. Ant.*, Vol. X., p. 101.

The latest of Rámachandra's inscriptions, and the last of his dynasty that is at present known to be extant, is dated in Saka 1220 (A.D. 1298-9). But, prior to that date, there had commenced the course of events which led to the entire subversion of the power of the Yádavas of Devagiri. For the history of these events, as well as for all that we know about Samkara and Bhima, the sons, and Harapála, or perhaps Haripála, the son-in-law, of Rámachandra, we must turn to the chronicle of Ferishta.[1] And, as the account is that of the complete extinction of the last of the ancient Hindu dynasties of Western India, it is worthy of being given in some detail.

In A.D. 1294, Allá-ud-din,—the nephew, and subsequently the successor, of Jelál-ud-din, the first of the Khilji emperors of Delhi, —with the permission of the king, collected a body of eight thousand chosen horse at Karrah-Mánikpur on the Ganges, which was the seat of his government, and set out to invade the Dekkan. Crossing the Narmadá, which was then the northern boundary of the Devagiri kingdom, he proceeded by way of Ellichpur, and pressed on by forced marches till he arrived in the neighbourhood of Devagiri itself. Rámachandra, or Rámadeva as he is called in the Muhammadan chronicle, collected such forces as he could muster on the spur of the moment, and opposed the invaders at a distance of about four miles from his capital. But, being defeated, he was forced to retire into the hill-fort above the city, and the city itself was easily taken, entered, and pillaged by Allá-ud-din's troops. Allá-ud-din having given out that his force was only the advance-guard of the emperor's army,—the neighbouring chiefs, each busy with his own preparations for defence, were prevented from coalescing with Rámachandra against the invaders; and Rámachandra, seeing that he must soon be obliged to surrender, and apprehending that the king of Delhi intended to make an entire conquest of the Dekkan, became anxious to secure peace before any other forces arrived. He accordingly offered a large amount of gold and jewels, sufficient, with the booty that Allá-ud-din had already obtained, to indemnify him for the expenses of his expedition; and his proposals were accepted by Allá-ud-din, who released his prisoners, and promised to quit the town on the morning of the fifteenth day from his first entrance. Meanwhile Rámachandra's son, Samkara, who, on the first appearance of the enemy, had retired to collect troops, advanced with a large army to within a few miles of the city. Rámachandra sent word to him that peace had been concluded. But Samkara, relying on the numerical superiority of his forces, disregarded the injunctions of his father, and sent a message to Allá-ud-din, calling on him to restore whatever plunder he had taken and to leave the province quietly. Thereupon Allá-ud-din left a force of a thousand horse to invest the fort and to prevent a sally, and marched with the rest of his army to attack Samkara. A battle ensued, in which the Muhammadan troops, overpowered by

---

1 Briggs' translation, Vol. I., pp. 304 to 420; see also Elphinstone's *History of India*, Cowell's edition, pp. 386 to 408. My account is of course only an abstract; but I have found it convenient in many places to use the actual words of Ferishta as rendered by his translator.

numbers, fell back on all sides. They were joined, however, by the force which had been left to invest the fort. And the Hindus, prevented by the dust from discovering the numbers of this force, supposed that the king's army, of which they had heard, had arrived. A panic seized them, and they broke and fled in all directions. Allá-ud-din did not think it prudent to pursue them, but returned and again invested the fort. Rámachandra now found himself to be in great difficulties; especially because a number of bags, supposed to contain grain, which had been taken into the fort for the support of the garrison, were found to contain only salt. He accordingly again commenced negociations, and peace was ultimately concluded, the terms being that Allá-ud-din should receive, on evacuating the country, "six hundred *maunds* of pearls, two *maunds* of diamonds, rubies, emeralds, and sapphires, one thousand *maunds* of silver, and four thousand pieces of silk, besides," says Ferishta, "a long list of other precious commodities, to which reason forbids us to give credit." Also the cession of Ellichpur and its dependencies was demanded, that Allá-ud-din might leave there a garrison for the collection of the revenues which were to be remitted to him at Karrah-Mánikpur. Allá-ud-din accordingly released all his prisoners, and, on the twenty-fifth day from his first arrival before Devagiri, marched in triumph out of the city and proceeded on his return to Karrah.

It was shortly after these events that Allá-ud-din inveigled the king, Jelál-ud-din, into meeting him, with only a small retinue, at Mánikpur. On the 19th July, A. D. 1295, Jelál-ud-din was treacherously murdered there by Allá-ud-din's adherents. And Allá-ud-din then ascended the throne of Delhi.

For some years after this, the Yádavas of Devagiri remained unmolested. But, Rámachandra having become irregular in the payment of his tribute, in A.D. 1306 Allá-ud-din placed an army of a hundred thousand horse under the command of one of his eunuchs, Malik Káfur, and sent him to subdue the Dekkan. The expedition was reinforced on its way by the troops of Ain-ul-Mulk Multáni, the governor of Málwá, and of Alaf Khán, the governor of Gujarát; and one of the principal objects of it was to recover Devaladevi, the daughter of Kauladevi who, on the defeat and flight of her husband, Karnaráya of Gujarát,[1] in A.D. 1297, had been taken into the harem of Allá-ud-din and had become a favourite with him. Karnaráya, taking Devaladevi with him, had fled to Bágláns,[2] one of the districts dependent on Gujarát and bordering on the Devagiri dominions. He refused the demand of Malik Káfur that she should be given up, and eventually, listening to overtures from Devagiri, promised her, then in her thirteenth year, in marriage to Samkara. Karnaráya, however, was shortly after this attacked by a division of the army under Alaf Khán, and, being totally defeated, fled to Devagiri. Bhimadeva, the brother of Samkara, who had conducted the negociations for the marriage, and

1 Apparently Karnadeva II., the last of the Vyághrapalli or Vághelá branch of the Chaulukyas of Anhilwád; *Ind. Ant.*, Vol. VI., p. 213.

2 Bágláns, with Chándor as its capital, appears to have been subsequently the north-west division of the province of Aurangábád.

who with only a small retinue was conveying Devaladevi to Devagiri, was intercepted by a small body of Alaf Khán's troops, and, in the skirmish that ensued, Devaladevi was captured and taken to Alaf Khán's camp. Alaf Khán straightway returned with her to Delhi; and she was soon after married to Allá-ud-din's eldest son, Khizr Khán.

Malik Káfur, however, went on into the Dekkan, and, having subdued a great part of the Maráthá country, which he distributed among his officers, proceeded to the siege of Devagiri. But Rámachandra, being in no condition to make successful opposition, left Samkara in the fort, and advanced with presents to meet the conqueror, in order to obtain peace. Malik Káfur, accordingly, drew up an account of his expedition and sent it to the king, and, some time after took Rámachandra with him to Delhi, with rich presents, to pay his respects. Rámachandra was received there with great marks of favour and distinction, and royal dignities were conferred upon him; and, not only was he restored to his government, but other districts were added to his dominions, for all of which he did homage and paid tribute to the king of Delhi. The king, on this occasion, gave him the district of Nausári, near Gujarát, as a personal estate, and a *lac* of *tankas* to pay his expenses home. For the rest of his life Rámachandra did not neglect to send the annual tribute to Delhi.

In A.D. 1309, Rámachandra entertained Malik Káfur and Khwájá Háji at Devagiri, where they halted on their way to subdue the king of Worangal.

In A.D. 1310, Allá-ud-din, as has been mentioned in the preceding section, sent Malik Káfur and Khwájá Háji with a large army to reduce the Hoysalas of Dvárasamudra. Having reached Devagiri, they found that Rámachandra was dead, and that Samkara was not well affected to the Muhammadans. Leaving a part of his army at Paithán on the Godávari, to overawe Samkara and hold him in check, Malik Káfur continued his march to the south, and, having effected the conquest of Dvárasamudra, where the reigning king was Ballála III., returned to Delhi in A.D. 1311, apparently without having found any cause for the time being for active operations against Samkara. But Samkara subsequently withheld his tribute. Accordingly, in A.D. 1312, Malik Káfur for the fourth time proceeded into the Dekkan, and seized Samkara and put him to death. He then laid waste Maháráshtra and the Karnátaka, from Chaul[1] and Dábhol[2] on the coast as far as Mudgal[3] and Raichur,[4] and took up his residence at Devagiri, from which place he realised the tribute from the princes of Telingana and the Karnátaka, and remitted it to Delhi.

Soon after this, however, Malik Káfur was summoned up to Delhi, and, while he was occupied in intrigues there, Harapála or Haripála, the son-in-law of Rámachandra, stirred up the Dekkan to

---

1 Lat. 18° 34′ N., Long. 72° 59′ E.; twenty-five miles south of Bombay, in the present A'libág or Kolába District.

2 Lat. 17° 35′ N., Long. 73° 17′ E.; eighty miles south of Bombay, in the Ratnágiri District.

3 Lat. 16° 1′ N., Long. 76° 30′ E.; in the Nizám's Dominions.

4 Lat. 16° 12′ N., Long. 77° 26′ E.; in the Nizám's Dominions.

arms, expelled a number of the Muhammadan garrisons, and asserted his power over the former territories of Devagiri. The intrigues at Delhi ended in the death of Allá-ud-din, said to have been caused by poison administered by Malik Káfur, on the 19th December A.D. 1316. But shortly after this, Malik Káfur himself was assassinated, and Mubárik, the third son of Allá-ud-din was placed on the throne. In A.D. 1318, Mubárik himself led an army to chastise Harapála. On the arrival of the king, Harapála and his adherents fled. But a detachment was sent in pursuit of them, and Harapála was captured, brought back, flayed alive, and decapitated, and his head was set up over the gate of his own capital. This completed the extinction of the Yádava dynasty.

Up to A.D. 1338, Devagiri seems to have not been looked upon as a place of much importance, though it was the scene of many of the contests that ensued between the Muhammadans and the Maráthás during the completion of the subjugation of the Dekkan. But, in that year, Muhammad Tughlak, who had ascended the throne of Delhi in A.D. 1325, visited Devagiri on one of his campaigns, and was so much pleased with the situation and strength of the place, and considered it to be in so much more central a position than Delhi itself, that he decided upon making it the capital of his empire. He changed its name from Devagiri, or 'the mountain of the gods', to Daulatábád, or 'the city of wealth,' which name it still retains. But, though he three times compelled the population of Delhi to migrate to Daulatábád, his project of making it the capital of the empire failed in the end. Since the time of its change of name, however, Devagiri or Daulatábád has continued to be a Muhammadan town. In about A.D. 1342, it was visited by Ibn Batuta, a traveller from Tangiers, who describes the city as consisting then of three parts,—Daulatábád, Kataka (probably the citadel), and Dwaikir or Devagiri.[1]

---

[1] *Ind. Ant.*, Vol. III., p. 116.

SECTION X.

THE RATTAS OF SAUNDATTI AND BELGAUM.

We have been occupied hitherto with the history of the supreme dynasties, noticing only incidentally the great feudatory families of *Mahámandalesvaras,* through whom,—in addition to their *Mahápradhánas, Pradhánas, Senápatis,* and *Dandanáyakas,*—the sovereigns paramount carried on the administration of their dominions. We have now to deal in detail with these feudatory families, the members of which enjoyed a *status* very different from that of the other officials just named, inasmuch as,—instead of being only individual officers, of haphazard origin, selected for their personal abilities and invested with special powers,—they were the hereditary governors of different provinces of the kingdom, subordinate to whatever dynasty happened at the time to exercise the supreme sway.

The dynasty of the Ráshtrakutas died out, as we have seen, in the person of Kakka III. or Kakkala, in Saka 895 (A.D. 973-4). They left, however, an impress of their power and dominion in this part of the country, which long survived themselves, in the Ratta *Mahámandalesvaras,* who, for about three and a half centuries, —first as the feudatories of the Ráshtrakutas, then as the feudatories of the Western Chálukyas, and then apparently of their own independent authority until they were conquered by the Yádavas of Devagiri, — had the government of the Kundi or Kuhundi Three-thousand province, a division of the Kuntala country, which included the greater part of the Belgaum District and the south-western parts of the Kaládgi District. Their capital was first Sugandhavarti, the modern Saundatti [1] in the Belgaum District, and afterwards Venugráma or Velugráma, the modern Belgaum itself; and their inscriptions are found at those two places, and at Watnál, Sogal, Mutwád, Nesargi, Hannikeri, Konnur, Kalhole, and Bhoj, in the Belgaum District,—at Khánápur and Ráyabág in the Kolhápur State,—and at Lokápur on the highroad between Belgaum and Kaládgi.

In some of their inscriptions the members of this family call themselves Ráshtrakutas; and in one or two passages they assert that they belonged to the lineage of Krishna II. of that dynasty. But in the majority of instances they use the name of Ratta; and, though they may possibly have been of the same original stock with the Ráshtrakutas, the probability is that they were only some local division of the Reddi caste. They were of the Jain religion. They had the title of *Lattalur-puravar-ádhisvara* or *Lattanur-puravar-ádhisvara,* 'supreme lord of Lattalur or Lattanur, the best of cities;'

---

1 Lat. 15° 47' N., Long. 75° 12' E.; the chief town of the Parasgad Táluká.

but this city, which was therefore the place from which they originally started, has not yet been identified. They were entitled to carry the banner of a golden Garuda,[1] and to use the mark of red-lead or vermilion.[2] What the latter was, I have not been able to determine; but, as to the former, the only copper-plate grant of this family that has been discovered has on its seal a human figure, kneeling on its right knee, which must be Garuda. They were also entitled to have the musical instrument called *trivali* played before them.

The following is the Ratta genealogy :—

- Merada.
  - Prithvirâma. (Saka 797.)
    - Pittuga.
      - Sântivarmâ. (Saka 902.)
        - ⋮
        - Nanna.
          - Kârtavirya I. (Saka 902.)
            - Dâvari, or Dâyima.
            - Kannakaira I.
              - Erega.
                - Sena I.
                  - Kannakaira II. (Saka 1004 and 1018.)
                  - Kârtavirya II. (Saka 1009 and 1018.)
                    - Sena II.
                      - Kârtavirya III. (Saka 1065 and 1086.)
                        - Lakshmideva I. (Saka 1130.)
                          - Kârtavirya IV. (Saka 1121 and 1140.)
                            - Lakshmideva II. (Saka 1150.)
                          - Mallikârjuna. (Saka 1123 and 1130.)
              - Anka. (Saka 970.)

1 *Suvarnagarudadhvaja.*

2 *Sinduralânchhana.*

Merada and his son, Prithvirâma, were originally teachers, of the Káreya sect of the holy Mailápatirtha. Prithvirâma was the first of the family to be invested with the rank and authority of a *Mahásámanta* or *Mahámandalesvara*,—by the Ráshtrakuta king Krishna II., about Saka 797 (A.D. 875-6).[1] **Merada, and Prithvirâma.**

Of Pittuga, the son of Prithvirâma, we have no record, except that he confronted and repulsed a certain Ajavarmá, who came to attack him, and that his wife was Nijikabbe or Nijiyabbe. Of the time of his son, Sántivarmá or Sánta, whose wife was Chandikabbe, we have one inscription, at Saundatti, dated Saka 902 (A.D. 980-1) the Vikrama *samvatsara*.[2] It mentions him as the feudatory of the Western Chálukya king Taila II., but does not give any further historical information about him. **Pittuga, and Sántivarmá.**

After Sántivarmá there is a break in the genealogy, there being nothing to show whether Nanna was his uncle or brother, or in what way he was related to him. Of Nanna, also called Nannapayyarána, we have no details. Of the time of his son, Kártavirya I. or Katta I., there is one inscription, at Sogal near Saundatti. It is of the same date as the inscription of his predecessor, Sántivarmá, *viz.* Saka 902 (A.D. 980-1), and records that he was governing the Kundi country as the feudatory of the Western Chálukya king Taila II. Another and later inscription speaks of him again as the feudatory of Taila II., who is mentioned therein by his title of A'havamalla I., and also records that it was he who fixed the boundaries of the Kuhundi or Kundi country. **Nanna, and Kártavirya I.**

Of Dávari or Dáyima, Kannakaira I. or Kanna I., and Erega or Eraga, we have no inscriptions or historical information. Of the time of Anka there are two inscriptions,—at Saundatti. One of them is the first part of a tablet which also bears a later inscription; it is dated Saka 970 (A.D. 1048-9), the Sarvadhári *samvatsara*, and records that he was the feudatory of the Western Chálukya king Somesvara I. The other is a fragment of the same date. **Dávari, Kannakaira I., Erega, and Anka.**

Of Sena I. or Kálasena I., and his wife Mailaladevi, we have no details. His eldest son, Kannakaira II. or Kanna II., is mentioned as one of the feudatory *Mahámandalesvaras* in the Tidgundi grant, from the Kaládgi District, of the Western Chálukya king Vikramáditya VI., which is dated Saka 1004 (A.D. 1082-3), the Dundubhi *samvatsara*.[3] He is also mentioned as the feudatory of the same king and of his son Jayakarna, in an inscription at Konnur in the Belgaum District, dated Saka 1009 (A.D. 1087-8), the Prabhava *samvatsara*.[4] And he seems to have been alive, and to have continued in authority in conjunction with his younger brother Kártavirya II., up to Saka 1018 (A.D. 1096-7), the Dhátu *samvatsara*; as he is mentioned, after the record of that date, in one of the Saundatti inscriptions.[5] **Sena I., and Kannakaira II.**

---

1 *Jour. Bo. Br. R. As. Soc.*, Vol. X., p. 194; and *P. S. and O.-C. Inscriptions*, No. 88.
2 *Jour. Bo. Br. R. As. Soc.*, Vol. X., p. 204. 3 *Ind. Ant.*, Vol. I., p. 80.
4 *Jour. Bo. Br. R. As. Soc.*, Vol. X., p. 287; *P. S. and O.-C. Inscriptions*, No. 93.
5 *Id.*, p. 194; *P. S. and O.-C. Inscriptions*, No. 88.

Kártavirya II.

Of the time of Kártavirya II. or Katta II.,—also called Senana-Singa, or 'the lion of Sena,'—and his wife Bhágaladevi, we have four inscriptions,—a fragment at Saundatti, the date of which is lost, but the preamble of which shows that he had held office under the Western Chálukya king Somesvara II.;[1] another at Saundatti, which is dated Saka 1009 (A.D. 1087-8), the Prabhava *samvatsara*; one at Watnál, which is dated in either the same or the following year; and the above-mentioned Saundatti inscription of Saka 1018 (A.D. 1096-7).

Sena II., and Kártavirya III.

Of Sena II. or Kálasena II., and his wife Lakshmidevi, we have no details. Of the time of Kártavirya III. or Kattama, and his wife Padmaladevi or Padmávati, we have four inscriptions,—two at Khánápur in the Kolhápur State, dated Saka 1065 (A.D. 1143-4), the Rudhirodgári *samvatsara*, and Saka 1084 (A.D. 1162-3), the Chitrabhánu *samvatsara*;[2] one at Bail-Hongal in the Belgaum District, dated Saka 1086 (A.D. 1164-5), the Tárana *samvatsara*;[3] and one at Konnur, the date of which is effaced.[4] In the first, he is spoken of as the feudatory of the Western Chálukya king Jagadekamalla II., and in the third, as being, or rather having been, the feudatory of Taila III. of the same dynasty. But in the fourth he has the title of *chakravarti*, or 'universal emperor.' From this, and from the fact that his descendants, though they retain the title of *Mahámandalesvara*, speak of themselves as enjoying *sámrájya*, or 'complete sovereignty,' and do not give the names of any paramount sovereigns in their inscriptions, it is plain that, in the time of Sena II. or of Kártavirya III., the Rattas established their independence, taking advantage of the general confusion that must have prevailed during the last few years of the Chálukya dynasty, in the occurrence of the events that finally ended in the complete subversion of it by Bijjala of the Kalachuri family.

Lakshmideva I.

Of Lakshmideva I., Lakshmana, or Lakshmidhara, whose wife was Chandaladevi or Chandrikádevi, we have one inscription,—at Hannikeri near Sampgaum, dated Saka 1130 (A.D. 1208-9), the Vibhava *samvatsara*. It is in this inscription that we first find that the capital of the Rattas was moved from Sugandhavarti to Venugráma, and that, in addition to the Kundi Three-thousand, they possessed also the Venugráma Seventy, a district which they appear to have acquired by conquest from the Kádambas of Goa. This inscription speaks of Lakshmideva I. as a descendant of the Ráshtrakuta king Krishna II. to whom it gives the title of *Kandhára-puravar-ádhisvara*, or 'supreme lord of Kandhárapura, the best of cities.' This may have been one of the original cities of the Ráshtrakutas; but the present mention of it is an isolated one.

Kártavirya IV., and Mallikárjuna.

Of the time of Kártavirya IV., and his brother Mallikárjuna, who reigned conjointly with him as *Yuvarája*, we have seven inscriptions,—one at Sankeswar near Chikkodi, dated Saka 1121 (A.D. 1199-1200), the Siddhárthi *samvatsara*, and Saka 1124, the Dundubhi *samvatsara*;[5] one at Ráyabág, dated Saka 1124 for Saka 1123

---

1 *Jour. Bo. Br. R. As. Soc.*, Vol. X., p. 213.

2 Elliot *MS. Collection*, Vol. II., pp. 547 and 548.

3 See *Ind. Ant.*, Vol. IV., p. 115.

4 *P. S. and O.-C. Inscriptions*, No. 94; see the *Third Archæological Report*, p. 103.

5 Elliot *MS. Collection*, Vol. II., p. 561.

(A.D. 1201-2), the Durmati *samvatsara;* [1] two, which were formerly at Belgaum but were removed from there and have now been entirely lost sight of, dated Saka 1127 for Saka 1126 (A.D. 1204-5), the Raktákshi *samvatsara;* [2] one at Kalhole near Gokák, of the same date; [3] one, a copper-plate grant, at Bhoj near Chikkodi, dated Saka 1131 for Saka 1130 (A.D. 1208-9), the Vibhava *samvatsara;* and one at Nesargi near Sampgaum, dated Saka 1141 for Saka 1140 (A.D. 1218-9), the Bahudhánya *samvatsara.*[4] From the dates of his earlier inscriptions, it is plain that Kártavirya IV. first shared the government with his father Lakshmideva I. His wives were Echaladevi and Mádevi or Mahádevi.

Lakshmideva II.

Of the time of Lakshmideva II., also called Boppana-Singa, or 'the lion of Boppa,' we have only one inscription,—at Saundatti; it is dated Saka 1151 for Saka 1150 (A.D. 1228-9), the Sarvadhári *samvatsara.* [5] This is the last notice that we have of the Rattas. Lakshmideva II. seems to have been the last of his race, and to have succumbed to the rising power of the Yádavas of Devagiri. By Saka 1150 we find Singhana II. of that dynasty making grants and setting up inscriptions in the neighbourhood of Kolhápur, in the Kaládgi District, in the Toragal Six-thousand, in the Belvola country, and in Dhárwád and Maisur, in sufficient numbers to show that the whole of the country on the north, east, and south of the Kundi Three-thousand was then entirely subject to him; though, as is shown by the date of the inscription of Lakshmideva II., he had evidently left the Rattas unmolested up to then. In Saka 1171 (A.D. 1249-50), however, we find Singhana's son Krishna in possession of the Kundi Three-thousand. It must have been, therefore, in the latter part of Singhana's reign that the Rattas were subjugated by his minister and general Vichana, as recorded in the Behatti grant of Krishna dated Saka 1175.[6]

---

1 Elliot *MS. Collection*, Vol. II., p. 564; and see *Jour. Bo. Br. R. As. Soc.*, Vol. X., p. 182.
2 Elliot *MS. Collection*, Vol. II., pp. 571 and 576.
3 *Jour. Bo. Br. R. As. Soc.*, Vol. X., p. 220; *P. S. and O.-C. Inscriptions*, No. 95.
4 *Id.*, Vol. X., p. 240.
5 *Id.*, Vol. X., p. 260; *P. S. and O.-C. Inscriptions*, No. 89.
6 *Id.*, Vol. XII., p. 42.

SECTION XI.

THE KA'DAMBAS OF BANAWA'SI AND HA'NGAL.

As in the case of the Western Chalukyas and Chálukyas, so, in the case of the Kadambas and Kádambas, the difference in the first syllable of the name seems to imply that the Kádamba *Mahámandalesvaras* of Banawási and Hángal, and their relatives of Goa of whom we shall treat in the following Section, cannot claim a direct lineal descent from the early Kadamba kings of whom an account has been given in Section II. above.

The Kádambas of Banawási[1] and Hángal[2] deduce their origin from the three-eyed and four-armed Mayuravarmá I.,—the Mukkanna-Kadamba of one inscription,[3]—who was the son of the god Siva and the earth. This legend as to the birth of Mayuravarmá I., —taken in connection with the legend of the Kádambas of Goa, that the founder of their family, Jayanta or Trilochana-Kadamba, sprang from the earth at the foot of a *kadamba*-tree, where a drop of sweat fell from the forehead of Siva after the conquest of Tripura, —suggests the inference that the Kádambas, and perhaps the Kadambas before them, were an aboriginal race, and not one of the A'ryan tribes that immigrated from the north; especially if, as Mr. Rice intimates,[4] the *kadamba*-tree is one of the toddy-producing palms which are so common throughout the districts ruled over by the Kadambas and Kádambas.[5] At the same time it is worthy of notice that there is also a tradition that Mayuravarmá I., not simply introduced, but brought with him, twelve-thousand Bráhmans, of thirty-two *gotras*, purified by performing the *agnihotra*-sacrifice, from the *agrahára* of Ahichchhatra,[6] and established them in the

---

1 Lat. 14° 33′ N., Long. 75° 5′ E.; in the Sirsi Táluká of the North Kanara District.

2 Lat. 14° 46 N., Long. 75° 12′ E.; the chief town of the Táluká of the same name in the Dhárwád District.

3 *P. S. and O.-C. Inscriptions*, No. 221.

4 *Mysore Inscriptions*, p. xxxiii.

5 That liquor is distilled in some way or other from the *kadamba*-tree is shown by the legend in the *Vishnu-Purána*, V., xxv., where Váruni or Madirá, at the command of her husband Varuna, "established herself in the hollow of a *kadamba*-tree, in the woods of Vrindávana; and Baladeva, roaming about, came there, and, smelling the pleasant fragrance of liquor, resumed his ancient passion for strong drink" (*váruni; madirá*); Wilson's translation; Hall's edition, Vol. V., p. 65.—It is added in a footnote, "there is no vinous exudation from the *kadamba*-tree; but its flowers are said to yield a spirit, by distillation;—whence *kádambari* is one of the synonyms of wine or spirituous liquor."

6 There were evidently at least two places, whether regions or cities, called Ahichchhatra.—General Cunningham (*Archæological Reports*, Vol. I., p. 255) identifies one of them with the modern Rámnagar, about twenty-two miles to the north of Badaun in the North-West Provinces. While Prof. Lassen (*Map of Ancient India*) identifies apparently the same one with the modern Farokhábád, about fifty-five miles to the south-east of Badaun.—Prof. Hall (*Vishnu-Purána*, Vol. II., p. 161, note §) suggests that one of them was not far from the Vindhya mountains.—A Sinda inscription (*P. S. and O.-C. Inscriptions*, No. 86) records that Sinda, who was the son of Pulikála, and who was married to a Kadamba princess, was born at Ahichchhatra on the bank of the river Sindhu.—For other references, see *Ind. Ant.*, Vol. IX., p. 252, note.

agrahára of Sthánugudhapura or Tánagundur, the modern Tálgund or Táldagundi in the Shikárpur Táluká of the Sivamogga District of Maisur.[1]

The Kádambas of Banawási and Hángal were entitled to have the musical instrument called *permatti* played before them,—to carry the banner of a monkey, or perhaps of Hanumán, the king of monkeys,[2]—and to use the signet of a lion.[3] One of their family-titles was *Banavasi-puravar-ádhisvara*, or 'supreme lord of Banavási, the best of cities.' And their family-god was Vishnu, under the name of Madhukesvara of Jayantipura or Banawási.

The fullest account of the genealogy is given in a stone-tablet inscription at Kargudari in the Hángal Táluká of the Dhárwád District;[4] and, with a few additions from an inscription at Banawási,[5] another at Hángal,[6] and other sources, is as shown in the accompanying table. The Kargudari inscription states that Mayuravarmá I. was preceded by seventy-seven ancestors, who all reigned in succession; but as yet we have no further information regarding them. Including, as it does, a number of names as to which we have no historical data, it is of course open to doubt whether the list is altogether authentic; especially since the Ráshtrakuta inscriptions from Nidagundi, Kyásanur, Tálgund, and A'dur, all in the neighbourhood of Hángal, show that at any rate up to Saka 869 (A. D. 947-8) the Kádambas were preceded in the government of the Banavâse province by the members of another family of *Mahámandalesvaras*, called Chellaketana or Chellapatáka, whose history has still to be worked out.

Out of the annexed list of names, the first, in chronological order, of which we have any historical information, is that of Kirttivarmá II. or Kirttideva I., also called Tailana-Singa or 'the lion of Taila,' the son of Taila or Tailapa I. and Chávundaladevi. We find him in Saka 990 (A.D. 1068-9), the Kilaka *samvatsara*, governing the Banavâse Twelve-thousand, as the feudatory of the Western Chálukya king Somesvara I.[7] And in Saka 998 (A.D. 1076-7), the Nala *samvatsara*, and in Saka 999, the Pingala *samvatsara*, he was still governing the same district, as the feudatory of the Western Chálukya king Vikramáditya VI. Kirttivarmá II.

In Saka 1010 (A.D. 1088-9), the Vibhava *samvatsara*, we find Sántivarmá II., Sánta, or Sántaya, governing the Banavase Twelve-thousand and the Pánungal or Hángal Five-hundred, as the feudatory of Vikramáditya VI.[9] His wife was Siriyádevi, of the Pándya family. Sántivarmá II.

---

1 *P. S. and O.-C. Inscriptions*, No. 221.

2 *Sákhácharendradhvaja*; equivalent to *vánarendradhvaja*. Conf. the *vánaramahádhvaja* of the Kádambas of Goa.

3 *Simhalánchhana*. This was also used by the Kádambas of Goa, and appears on their coins and on the seals of their copper-plate grants. No coins or copper-plates of the Kádambas of Banawási and Hángal have been discovered yet.

4 *Ind. Ant.*, Vol. X., p. 249.

5 See *Id.*, Vol. IV., p. 206.

6 Elliot *MS. Collection*, Vol. II., p. 49; and *P. S. and O.-C. Inscriptions*, No. 90, where, on the authority of *Inscriptions in Dharwar and Mysore*, it is wrongly entered as being at Huli in the Belgaum District.—The original inscription appears to be not forthcoming now.

7 *Ind. Ant.*, Vol. IV., p. 206; and Elliot *MS. Collection*, Vol. I., p. 279.

8 *Ind. Ant.*, Vol. IV., p. 205; and Elliot *MS. Collection*, Vol. II., pp. 585 and 591.

9 Elliot *MS. Collection*, Vol. II., p. 594.

Tailapa II.

In Saka 1021 (A.D. 1099-1100), the Pramádi *samvatsara*, in Saka 1030 (A.D. 1108-9), the Sarvadhári *samvatsara*, in Saka 1044 (A.D. 1122-3), the Subhakrit *samvatsara*, and in Saka 1046 (A.D. 1124-5), the Krodhi *samvatsara*, we find Taila or Tailapa II. governing the Banavàse Twelve-thousand and the Pánungal Five-hundred, as the feudatory of Vikramáditya VI.[1] In the inscription of Saka 1030, his capital is called Pánthipura; this is only another name of Hángal, which in the inscriptions of this period is also called Virátakote and Virátanagara. His wives were Báchaladevi, of the Pándya family, and Chámaladevi, who was the mother of Tailama. Taila II. appears to have died in Saka 1057 (A.D. 1135-6), the Rákshasa *samvatsara*, during, or soon after, a siege of Hángal by the Hoysalas under Vishnuvardhana.[2] The Banawási and Hángal districts were then subjugated for the time being by Vishnuvardhana; but they were not retained by him for long.

Mayuravarmá III.

In Saka 1053 (A.D. 1131-2), the Virodhikrit *samvatsara*, Mayuravarmá III. was governing the Banavàse Twelve-thousand and the Hángal Five-hundred, presumably in conjunction with his father Tailapa II., as the feudatory of the Western Chálukya king Somesvara III.[3]

Mallikárjuna I.

In Saka 1054 (A.D. 1132-3), the Paridhávi *samvatsara*, presumably in conjunction with his father Tailapa II., and in Saka 1057 (A.D. 1135-6), the Rákshasa *samvatsara*, after his father's death, Mallikárjuna I., also called Tribhuvanamallarasa, another son of Tailapa II., was governing the Banavàse Twelve-thousand and the Pánungal Five-hundred, as the feudatory of Somesvara III.,[4] —and again in Saka 1066 (A.D. 1144-5), the Raktákshi *samvatsara*, as the feudatory of Jagadekamalla II.[5]

Kámadeva.

And in Saka 1111 (A.D. 1189-90), the Saumya *samvatsara*, Kámadeva or Kávadeva, also called Tailamana-Ankakára or 'the warrior or champion of Tailama,' was governing the Banavase Twelve-thousand, the Pánungal Five-hundred, and the Puligere or Lakshmeswar Three-hundred, as the feudatory of the Western Chálukya king Somesvara IV.,[6] after subjugating the countries of Male, Tulu, the Konkanas, and the Western Ghauts. Kámadeva's wife was Ketaladevi. There are two other inscriptions of Kámadeva, at Hángal.[7] One of them is dated in the sixteenth year of his reign, the Nala *samvatsara*, *i.e.* Saka 1118 (A.D. 1196-7); which gives Saka 1103 (A.D. 1181-2), the Sárvari *samvatsara*, as his initial date. This inscription is on a *viragal* or monumental tablet, the sculptures on which are a very vivid representation of battle-scenes. It records that in Saka 1118 the Hoysala king Vira-Ballála or Ballála II. came and pitched his camp at the A'nikere, the large tank on the west side of Hángal, and thence besieged the city. He was defeated, and repulsed for the time, by Kámadeva's forces under his generals Sohani and his son Padmayya or Padmana, the former of whom was

---

1 *Ind. Ant.*, Vol. X., p. 249; and Elliot *MS. Collection*, Vol. I., pp. 599 and 609, and Vol. II., p. 596.

2 Elliot *MS. Collection*, Vol. I., pp. 723 and 725.

3 *Id.*, Vol. I., pp. 634, 703, and 706.

4 *Id.*, Vol. I., pp. 637, 723, 725, and 727.

5 *Id.*, Vol., I., p. 772.

6 See note 6, p. 85.

7 *P. S. and O.-C. Inscriptions*, Nos. 106 and 107; Elliot *MS. Collection*, Vol. II., p. 605.

GENEALOGY OF THE KA'DAMBAS OF BANAWA'SI AND HA'NGAL.

Mayuravarmá I.
- Krishnavarmá.
- Nágavarmá I.
- Vishnuvarmá.
- Mrigavarmá.
- Satyavarmá.
- Vijayavarmá.
- Jayavarmá I.
- Nágavarmá II.
- Sántivarmá I.
- Kirttivarmá I.
- A'dityavarmá.
- Chattaya, Chatta, or Chattuga.
- Jayavarmá II., or Jayasimha.

Sons of Jayavarmá II.:
- **Mávulideva.**
- Taila I., or Tailapa I.
  - Kirttivarmá II., or Kirttideva I. (Saka 990 and 999.)
- Sántivarmá II., Sánta, or Sántaya. (Saka 1010.)
  - Taila II., or Tailapa II. (Saka 1021 and 1057.)
    - Mayuravarmá III. (Saka 1053.)
    - Mallikárjuna I. (Saka 1054 and 1057.)
    - Tailama.
      - Kirttideva II.
      - Kámadeva. (Saka 1103 and 1125.)
- Chokideva, or Jokideva.
- Vikrama, or Vikramánka.

killed in the battle. But Ballála II. seems to have soon afterwards completely subjugated the Kádambas and annexed their territory. There are inscriptions at Sátenhalli in the Kod Táluká which show that Kámadeva was still making active resistance, though he had apparently lost Hángal itself, in Saka 1125 (A.D. 1203-4), the Rudhirodgári *samvatsara*;[1] but what became of him after that date is not yet known.

In addition to the above, there are several detached names, the owners of which claim to belong to the family of the Kádambas of Banawási and Hángal, and about whom we have historical information, though they cannot as yet be referred to their places in the annexed genealogy. Thus, in Saka 941 (A.D. 1019-20), the Siddhárthi *samvatsara*, the *Mahámandalesvara* Kundamarasa, also called Kundamarasa. Sattigana-Chatta,[2] was governing the Banavása Twelve-thousand, the Sántalige Thousand which would seem to have been somewhere in the north or north-west of Maisur, and the Hayve Five-hundred or the country between Banawási and Balagámve and the sea, up to the borders of the western ocean, at his capital of Balipura or Balagámve, as the feudatory of the Western Chálukya king Jayasimha III.[3] In Saka 956 (A.D. 1034-5), the Bháva *samvatsara*, in Saka 960 (A.D. 1038-9), the Bahudhánya *samvatsara*, and in Saka 966 Mayuravarmá II. (A.D. 1044-5), the Tárana *samvatsara*, the *Mahámandalesvara* Mayuravarmá II. was governing the Pánungal Five-hundred, as the feudatory first of Jayasimha III. and then of Somesvara I.[4] In Saka 967 (A.D. 1045-6), the Párthiva *samvatsara*, in Saka 969, the Sarvajit Chávundaráya. *samvatsara*, and in Saka 970, the Sarvadhári *samvatsara*, the *Mahámandalesvara* Chávundaráya was governing the Banavási Twelve-thousand at his capital of Balligáve or Balagámve, as the feudatory of Somesvara I.[5] In Saka 977 (A.D. 1055-6), the Manmatha *samvatsara*, the *Mahámandalesvara* Harikesari was governing the Harikesari. Banavási Twelve-thousand, as the feudatory of Vikramáditya VI., who was then the viceroy for the above district and that of the Gangavádi Ninety-six-thousand.[6] In Saka 989 (A.D. 1067-8), the Plavamga *samvatsara*, the *Mahámandalesvara* Soyimarasa was Soyimarasa. governing the Pánungal Five-hundred, as the feudatory of Somesvara I.[7] In Saka 1092 (A.D. 1070-1), the Vikriti *samvatsara*, Nágatiyarasa or Nágáditya, and his son Ketarasa, the lord of Uchchangigiri, Nágatiyarasa, and Ketarasa. were governing a One-thousand district, which was probably the Sántalige Thousand, in subordination to the *Mahámandalesvara* Vijayapándya, of the Pándya family, who had acknowledged allegiance to the Western Chálukya king Taila III. up to Saka 1084, but who must have been independent at the time of this inscription.[8] In Saka 1163 (A.D. 1241-2), the Plava *samvatsara*, and Saka 1173 (A.D. 1251-2), the Virodhikrit *samvatsara*, the *Mahámandalesvara*

---

1 Elliot *MS. Collection*, Vol. II., pp. 309, 322, and 323.

2 Sattiga is another form of the name Satyásraya. In the present instance it denotes the Western Chálukya king Satyásraya II.

3 *Ind. Ant.*, Vol. V., p. 15.

4 Elliot *MS. Collection.*, Vol. I., pp. 57, 65, and 80.

5 *Id.*, Vol. I., pp. 91 and 99; and *Ind. Ant.*, Vol. IV., p. 179.

6 *Ind. Ant.*, Vol. IV., p. 203.

7 Elliot *MS. Collection*, Vol. I., p. 176. See also under Somadeva, the last name in the Section.

8 *P. S. and O.-C. Inscriptions*, No. 118.

Viramallideva, or Mallikárjuna II.

Vira-Mallideva or Mallikárjuna II. was governing the Banavási Twelve-thousand and the Pánungal Five-hundred, apparently independently;[1] and his initial date is fixed as either Saka 1137 (A.D. 1215-6), the Yuva *samvatsara*, or Saka 1138, the Dhátu *samvatsara*, by two other inscriptions which, without specifying the Saka year, give the Khara *samvatsara*, which was Saka 1152, as both the fifteenth and the sixteenth year of his reign.[2] And finally there is the *Mahámandalesvara* Somadeva, Soyideva, or Sovideva, who was governing apparently the Pánungal Five-hundred in the Durmukha *samvatsara*, his second year, the Vilambi *samvatsara*, his fourth year, and the Vikári *samvatsara*, his fifth year;[3] but there is nothing in his inscriptions to enable us to refer them to the Saka era. It is possible that he is the same person as the Soyimarasa mentioned above, who, as the feudatory of Somesvara I., was governing the Pánungal Five-hundred in Saka 989 (A.D. 1067-8), the Plavamga *samvatsara*.

Somadeva.

---

1 Elliot *MS. Collection*, Vol. II., pp. 603 and 604.
2 *Id.*, Vol. II., pp. 600 and 601.
3 *Id.*, Vol. II., pp. 607 to 610.

SECTION XII.

THE KA'DAMBAS OF GOA.

There was another family of Kádamba *Mahámandalesvaras*, at Gopakapattana, Gopakapuri, Gove, or Goa, with a minor capital at Palásiká, Palasige, or Palasi, the modern Halsige or Halsi[1] in the Khānāpur Taluka of the Belgaum District. They were undoubtedly of the same original stock as the Kádambas of Banawási and Hángal, though no indication has yet been obtained as to the point at which the two genealogies may be joined. But the separation of the two families must be of considerable antiquity; as each branch has a different name for the founder of it, though it is possible that the two names may be shown hereafter to belong to one and the same person. The Kádambas of Banawási and Hángal derive their origin from the three-eyed and four-armed Mayuravarmá, the son of Siva and the earth. Whereas the Kádambas of Goa derive their origin from the three-eyed and four-armed Jayanta, otherwise called Trilochana-Kadamba, who sprang from a drop of sweat that fell to earth near the roots of a *kadamba*-tree from the forehead of the god Siva after the conquest of Tripura. There are some indications that they were preceded at Goa by a Konkana branch of the Siláhára family, the founder of which was Jhalaphulla, and the representative of which, in Saka 930 (A.D. 1008-9), was Ráhurája, the feudatory of the Western Chálukya king Satyásraya II.[2] This, however, is not as yet a certainty, and requires further investigation before it can be accepted as such. Neither as to this, nor as to how the Kádambas first came into the Belgaum District and the Goanese territory, have we as yet any definite information.

Like the Kádambas of Banawási and Hángal, the Kádambas of Goa had the family-title of 'supreme lord of Banavási, the best of cities,' and were entitled to have the musical instrument called *permatti* played before them,—to carry the banner of a monkey, [3]—and to use the signet of a lion, which appears on the seals of the two copper-plate grants of this family that have been discovered, and on the gold coins of Permádi and Jayakesi III.[4] Their family-god was Siva, under the name of Saptakotisvara.[5] Their inscriptions are found at Goa itself,—at Halsi, Golihalli, Bailur, Degámve, Kittur,

---

1 Lat. 15° 32′ N., Long. 74° 40′ E.

2 *Jour. Bo. Br. R. As. Soc.*, Vol. I., p. 209.

3 *Vánaramahádhvaja.*

4 *Jour. Bo. Br. R. As. Soc.*, Vol. X., Appendix, p. xxiv.

5 The temple of Saptakotisvara is said to be 'Narven' in Goa (*Id.*, p. xxv.) This is perhaps the 'Narva' of the maps, on the island of Piedade.—The image is said to have been re-established by Mádhaváchárya who, when he was the *Mahápradhána* of Harihara II. of Vijayanagara (about A.D. 1380), besieged Goa and expelled the Turushkas or Muhammadans (*Id.*, Vol. IX., p. 227).

and Gudikatti, in the Belgaum District,—and at Narendra in the Dhárwád District; and, contrary to the usual practice, they are generally dated in the Kaliyuga era instead of in the Saka era.[1] Their genealogy is as below :—

- Guhalla.
  - Shashthadeva I., Chatta, Chattala, or Chattaya. (Saka 929.)
    - Jayakesi I. (Saka 974.)
      - Vijayáditya I.
        - Jayakesi II. (Saka 1047.)
          - Permádi, or Sivachitta. (Saka 1069 to 1097.)
          - Vijayáditya II., or Vishnuchitta. (Saka 1069 and 1093.)
            - Jayakesi III. (Saka 1097 and 1110.)
              - Tribhuvanamalla.
                - Shashthadeva II. (Saka 1168 and 1172.)
                - A daughter, (*married to Kámadeva or Kávana.*)

Guhalla, Shashthadeva I., and Jayakesi I.

Of Guhalla, also called Vyághramári or 'the tiger-slayer,' we have no historical details. Shashthadeva I., Chatta, Chattala, or Chattaya, is mentioned in the Gudikatti inscription as being in Saka 929 (A.D. 1007-8), the Plavamga *samvatsara,* the feudatory of Jayasimha III. of the Western Chálukya dynasty; at that time Satyásraya II. was still reigning, and Jayasimha III., his nephew, can have been only his viceroy. The second part of the same inscription mentions Jayakesi I. as being in Saka 974 (A.D. 1052-3), the Nandana *samvatsara,* the feudatory of the Western Chálukya king Somesvara I. And it is in other places recorded of him that he slew the king of Kápardikadvipa, destroyed the Cholas, and uprooted Kámadeva,—that he assembled the Kádambas, conquered the Álupas, and established the Chálukyas in their kingdom,—that he caused the Chálukyas and the Cholas to become friends at Kánchi,—and that

[1] The initial date of the Kaliyuga is the vernal equinox of B.C. 3102 (*Ind. Ant.,* Vol. V., p. 152). For convenience of comparison with the other tables in this paper, Saka dates are substituted for the Kaliyuga dates in the genealogical table of this family.

he established himself at Gopakapattana as his capital. Kápardikadvipa is perhaps the island and adjoining territories of Shatshashti or Salsette, as named after Kapardi II., of the Konkana branch of the Siláháras, who was reigning in the Konkana in Saka 775 (A.D. 853-4) and Saka 799, in the time of the Ráshtrakuta king Amoghavarsha I.[1] And, if so, the king of Kápardikadvipa, slain by Jayakesi I., must be Nágárjuna, who was intermediate between Chhittarája (Saka 946) and Mummuni or Mumváni (Saka 982), and as to the events of whose reign the Siláhára inscriptions are silent. That the Siláháras met with some serious reverses in or about the time of Nágárjuna, is apparent from what is said of Anantapála or Anantadeva, the son of Nágárjuna; *viz.*, that "he cast into the ocean of the edge of his sword those wicked heaps of sin ...., who, at a time of misfortune from relatives that had become hostile, obtained power and devastated the whole of this Konkana district, harassing gods and Bráhmans."[2] In the *Dvyásrayakosha* of Hemachandra and Abhayatilaka, it is narrated that Karna I., of the dynasty of the Chaulukyas of Anhilwád, married Mayánalladevi the daughter of a Kádamba king Jayakesi who was ruling at Chandrapura in the Dekkan.[3] Karna's date being from A.D. 1063-4 to A.D. 1093-4,[4] this Jayakesi of Chandrapura seems to be the present Jayakesi I.; but Chandrapura has not been identifiied,—unless perchance, it is a Sanskritised form of Chandgad, the chief town of the Mahál of that name in the Belgaum District.

Of his son, Vijayáditya I. or Vijayárka I., the only definite record that we have is that his wife was Chattaladevi, the sister of Bijjaladevi who was the mother of Jagaddeva of the Sántara family of Patti-Pombuchchapura.[5] Vijayáditya I.

His son, Jayakesi II., who styles himself *Konkana-Chakravarti*, or 'universal emperor of the Konkanas,' was the contemporary, and in the inscriptions is called the 'elder brother' by courtesy for 'cousin,' of the Jagaddeva referred to above. The only inscription of his time that we have is a stone-tablet at Narendra, which is dated Saka 1047 (A.D. 1125-6), the Visvávasu *samvatsara*, while, as the feudatory of the Western Chálukya king Vikramáditya VI., he was governing the Konkana Nine-hundred, the Palasige Twelve-thousand, the Payve or Hayve Five-hundred, and the Kavadidvipa Lac-and-a-quarter, which would seem to be the Kápardikadvipa mentioned above and to include the northern provinces of the Konkanas.[6] In his earlier years he seems to have made an attempt to throw off the Chálukya supremacy; as it is to his time that we must refer the events which led to A'chugi II. of the Sinda family, another feudatory of Vikramáditya VI., taking Goa and giving it to the flames, and seizing upon the Konkana; and he is undoubtedly the Jayakesi whom Permádi I., the son of A'chugi II., met and put to flight. His quarrel with the Chálukyas, however, must have been Jayakesi II.

---

1 *Jour. Bo. Br. R. As. Soc.*, Vol. XIII., p. 11.
2 *Ind. Ant.*, Vol. IX., p. 37.—The full bearing of this passage cannot be determined till we obtain an explanation of *munapavanajushán* and *Vakulapatisakhá*.
3 *Id.*, Vol. IV., p. 233. 4 *Id.*, Vol. VI., p. 213.
5 *P. S. and O.-C. Inscriptions*, No. 180.
6 *Jour. Bo. Br. R. As. Soc.*, Vol. IX., p. 265.

soon and permanently made up again,[1] as Vikramáditya VI. gave him his daughter Mailaladevi in marriage.[2] Jayakesi II. was also at some time or other conquered by the Hoysala king Vishnuvardhana, who thereby acquired the Halasige or Palasige district;[3] but it must have been soon recovered by the Kádambas. Jayakesi II. also appears to be the *Mahámandalesvara* Jayakesi who is mentioned, in one of the Western Chálukya inscriptions at Lakshmeswar dated Saka 1069 (A.D. 1147-8), the Prabhava *samvatsara*, among the persons of distinction to whom presents were given at the time of making a grant to the god Somanátha.[4]

Permádi, and Vijayáditya II.

The sons of Jayakesi II. were Permádi, also called Perma and Paramardi, and Vijayáditya II., also called Vijayárka II. They also acquired respectively the names of Sivachitta and Vishnuchitta, by their devotion to the gods Siva and Vishnu. Permádi had also the title of *Malavara-mári*, 'the slayer of the Malavas, or the people of the Ghaut country,' which corresponds to *Malaparol-ganda*, one of the titles of the Hoysala dynasty. And Vijayáditya II. had also the title of Vánibhushana or Sarasvatibhushana. Permádi's wife was Kamaládevi. In one passage her father Kámadeva is said to be of the Somavamsa, or race of the moon, and her mother Chattaladevi to be of the Pándya family; while in another passage Kámadeva is said to be of the Suryavamsa, or race of the sun, and Chattaladevi to be of the Somavamsa. It was Kamaládevi who caused to be built the small but elaborately sculptured temple of the god Kamala-Náráyana and the goddess Mahálakshmi at Degámve, which contains three of the inscriptions of this family; it was constructed by Tippoja, the *sutradhári* or 'mason' of the god Bankesvaradeva, and the son of the *sutradhári* Holloja of Huvina-Báge or probably Ráyabág in the Kolhápur State, and by Tippoja's son Bágoja.[5] Vijayáditya's wife was Lakshmidevi, the daughter of a king Lakshmideva. The two brothers reigned conjointly, from Kaliyuga 4248 (Saka 1069; A.D. 1147-8), the Prabhava *samvatsara*. The earliest of their inscriptions, at Golihalli, is dated in the fourteenth year, the Vikrama *samvatsara* (Saka 1082; A.D. 1160-1), the seventeenth year, the Svabhánu *samvatsara* (Saka 1085; A.D. 1163-4), and the twenty-sixth year, the Nandana *samvatsara* (Saka 1094; A.D. 1172-3), of the reign of Permádi.[6] He was then, at his capital of Gove, ruling over the Konkana Nine-hundred, the Palasige Twelve-thousand, and the Venugráma or Belgaum Seventy. The Bailur inscription is dated in the twenty-first year of his reign, the Sarvajit *samvatsara*, which was Kaliyuga 4268 (Saka 1089; A.D. 1167-8), and also in his twenty-second year, the Sarvadhári *samvatsara*. In one of the Halsi inscriptions, we find him, in the twenty-third year of his reign, Kaliyuga 4270 (Saka 1091; A.D. 1169-70), the Virodhi *samvatsara*, making a grant of the village of Sindavalli in the Kálagiri *kampana*[7] of the Palasi district. In one of the Degámve inscriptions, we find him, in the twenty-eighth year of his reign,

1 The submission of Jayakesi is recorded in the *Vikramánkadevacharita*, V., 25.
2 She was the daughter of Vikramáditya VI. by his wife Malayamatidevi, and was the younger sister of Somesvara III. 3 *P. S. and O.-C. Inscriptions*, No. 232.
4 *Id.*, No. 97. 5 *Jour. Bo. Br. R. As. Soc.*, Vol. IX., p. 294. 6 *Id.*, p. 296.
7 *Id.*, p. 278.

Kaliyuga 4275 (Saka 1096; A.D. 1174-5), the Jaya *samvatsara*, reigning at Gopakapuri, and making a grant of the village of Degámve in the Degámve *kampana* of the Palásiká district.[1] And by another inscription at Golihalli, in Kaliyuga 4283, the Manmatha *samvatsara*, he and his mother Mailaladevi were reigning at Gove; the proper date of this inscription, however, seems to be Kaliyuga 4276 (Saka 1097; A. D. 1175-6), which was the Manmatha *samvatsara*, Kaliyuga 4283 being the Subhakrit *samvatsara*. Of Vijayáditya II. we have only one inscription; it is at Halsi, and is dated Kaliyuga 4270 for 4272 (Saka 1093; A.D. 1171-2), the Khara *samvatsara*, and the twenty-fifth year of his reign, and records the grant of the village of Bhalaká in the Kálagiri *kampana* of the Palasi district.[2] He appears to be the Vijayáditya who, in a Hoysala inscription at Balagámve, is mentioned as having been made to pay tribute by some chieftains who were subsequently the feudatories of the Hoysala king Ballála II.[3]

The succession was continued by Jayakesi III., who also had the title of *Malavara-mári*, the son of Vijayáditya II. Of his time we have two inscriptions,—a copper-plate grant at Halsi, which is dated, in the thirteenth year of his reign, in Kaliyuga 4288 (Saka 1109; A.D. 1187-8), to which, according to the Telinga computation, the Siddhárthi *samvatsara* is allotted, instead of the Plavamga *samvatsara*;[4] and a stone-tablet at Kittur, which is dated, in the fifteenth year of his reign, in Kaliyuga 4289 (Saka 1110; A.D. 1188-9), to which the Durmati *samvatsara* is allotted instead of the Kilaka *samvatsara*.[5] His inscriptions, taken with those of Permádi, fix Kaliyuga 4276 (Saka 1097; A.D. 1175-6), the Manmatha *samvatsara*, for the commencement of his reign. The first of his inscriptions records that he established the god A'divaráha in a temple in front of the already existing temple of Narasimha at Palásiká, and allotted to the idol the village of Kiri-Halasige, or the smaller Halasige, and a variety of other grants. His second inscription contains an interesting account of a trial by ordeal. There being a dispute between Sivasakti, the *A'chárya* or priest of the god Kallesvaradeva of Kittur, and Kalyánasakti, the *A'chárya* of the *Mulasthánadeva* or the 'original god of the locality,' regarding the ownership of a field,—the two contending parties met before the *Dandanáyaka* Isvara, and agreed to put it to the test of the *phaladivya* or 'ordeal by holding a red-hot ploughshare.' Accordingly, on Sunday the seventh day of the dark fortnight of the month A'shádha, they met again in the presence of the principal villagers of Degámve, assembled at the temple of the god Mallikárjuna of that village. And then Kalyánasakti, taking the sacred symbols on his head, declared that the field belonged to the *Mulasthánadeva*; while Sivasakti, holding a red-hot ploughshare in his hand, made oath that the field belonged to the god Kallesvara. On the following day, the principal villagers examined the hand of Sivasakti, and, presumably finding it uninjured, decided that he had won his cause, and that the field in dispute belonged to the god Kallesvara.

Jayakesi III.

---

[1] *Jour. Bo. Br. R. As. Soc.*, Vol. IX., pp. 266 and 287. [2] *Id.*, p. 280.
[3] *P. S. and O.-C. Inscriptions*, No. 192.
[4] *Jour. Bo. Br. R. As. Soc.*, Vol. IX., p. 241. [5] *Id.*, p. 304.

Tribhuvanamalla, and Shashthadeva II.

Of Tribhuvanamalla and his wife Mánikyádevi, we have no historical details. Of the time of his son Shashthadeva II., the last of the family as far as our present knowledge goes, we have one inscription,—a copper-plate grant from Goa, which is dated, in the fifth year of his reign, in Kaliyuga 4348 for 4351 (Saka 1172; A.D. 1250-1), the Sádhárana *samvatsara*; this fixes Kaliyuga 4347 (Saka 1168; A.D. 1246-7), the Prabhava *samvatsara*, as his initial date. It records a grant, at Goa itself, to the god Siva under the name of Govesvara. The grant is made by Shashthadeva II. in conjunction with a certain Kámadeva or Kávana,—the son of Lakshmideva and the brother-in-law of Shashthadeva himself,—who, both in the body of the inscription and on the seal of the plates, is called 'the establisher of Shashthadeva'.[1] It would seem, therefore, that the power of the Kádambas of Goa was then on its last legs, and that it died out with Shashthadeva II. In fact,—as the Venugráma Seventy district was, as we have already seen, in the possession of the Rattas in Saka 1130 (A.D. 1208-9); and as Vijayáditya, of the Kolhápur branch of the Siláhára family, is stated to have re-established the kings of Sthánakamandala, or Thánú, and of Gová, the former of whom certainly, and the latter of whom perhaps, belonged to the Konkana branches of his own family,—the probability is that the kingdom of the Kádambas of Goa was practically destroyed at the death of Jayakesi III., and that whatever power Shashthadeva II. enjoyed was only of a transitory and very limited nature.

---

1 *Sri-Shashthadeva-pratishthápakah Sri-Kámadeva-bhumipálah.*

SECTION XIII.

THE SINDAS OF ERAMBARAGE.

The Sindas, who have already been mentioned in connection with some of the Western Chálukya and the Hoysala kings, were another family of *Mahámandalesvaras* who played an important part in the history of these districts. Their inscriptions are found at Pattadakal, Arasibidi, and Aihole, in the Kaládgi District,—and at Naregal, Kodikop, Ron, and Sudi, in the Dhárwád District. Their capital was Erambarage or Erambirage, which is probably, as Sir Walter Elliot has suggested,[1] the modern 'Yelburga' or 'Yelboorga of the maps, in the Nizám's Dominions.[2] And they possessed the extreme south-west corner of the Nizám's Dominions, the southern parts of the Kaládgi District, and the north-east portion of the Dhárwád District, from the beginning to nearly the end of the twelfth century A.D.

The name of the founder of the family is not given in the inscriptions that have as yet been brought to notice. But the genealogy, as far as those inscriptions go, is as given in the accompanying table.

Of A'chugi I., or A'cha, and his successors, down to and inclusive of Singa II., we have no information beyond the bare mention of their names. A'chugi I., &c.

A'chugi II.,—also called A'cha, A'chi, A'chama, and Tribhuvanamalladevara-Kesari, or 'the lion of Tribhuvanamalladeva,'—was the feudatory of the Western Chálukya king Vikramáditya VI. His wife was Mádevi or Mahádevi. We have one inscription of his time,—at Kodikop, dated Saka 1044 (A.D. 1122-3), the Subhakrit *samvatsara*.[3] He was then governing the Kisukád[4] Seventy, and several other towns the chief of which was Nareyangal-Abbegere,[5] the chief town of the Nareyangal Twelve which was in the Belvola Three-hundred. His own inscription does not give any further historical information about him. But the later ones record that he was "a very handmill for grinding the wheat which was *(the race of)* Jaggu," and that he was the disgracer of Hallakavadikeya-Singa; that, at the command of his master, Vikramáditya VI., he pursued and prevailed against the Hoysalas, took Gove or Goa, put Lakshma to flight in war, caused the Pándyas to retreat, dispersed the Malapas or people of the Western Ghauts, and seized upon the Konkana; A'chugi II.

---

[1] *Madras Jour. of Lit. and Science*, Vol. VII., p. 207.

[2] Lat. 15° 37′ N., Long. 76° 5′ E.

[3] *Jour. Bo. Br. R. As. Soc.*, Vol. XI. p. 247.

[4] Lit. 'ruby-forest.' The name appears not to be known now; but it evidently denoted the country lying round Kisuvolal, lit. 'ruby-city,' or Pattada-Kisuvolal, *i.e.* Pattadakal.

[5] The modern Naregal, ten miles to the south by east from Ron,

that he gave Gove and Uppinakatti to the flames; and that he defeated, captured, and drove back Bhoja, who, with his troops, had invaded his country. This Bhoja must be the *Mahámandalesvara* Bhoja I. of the family of the Siláháras of Kolhápur, to be noticed in the next Section; and this repulse of Bhoja must have occurred at some time anterior to Saka 1031 (A.D. 1109-10),—probably about Saka 1020.

Permádi I.

Of the time of his eldest son Permádi I.,—also called Perma, Pemma, Paramardi, Hemmadi, and Jagadekamalla-Permádi,—we have four inscriptions, three at Naregal and one at Kodikop. Of the Naregal inscriptions, two only commemorate grants that had been made by village officers before his time.[1] The third is of his own time, and is dated Saka 1026 (A.D. 1104-5), the Tárana *samvatsara*.[2] The Kodikop inscription is dated Saka 1066 (A.D. 1144-5), the Raktákshi *samvatsara*.[3] His capital was Erambarage or Erambirage;[4] and he had the government of the Kisukád Seventy, the Kelavádi[5] Three-hundred, and the Nareyangal Twelve, as the feudatory, first of the Western Chálukya king Vikramáditya VI., and then of his son Jagadekamalla II. The inscriptions record of him that he vanquished Kulasekharánka, besieged Chatta, pursued Jayakesi, who must be the second of that name of the family of the Kádambas of Goa, and seized upon the royal power of the Hoysalas; and that he advanced to the mountain-passes of the marauder Bittiga, or the Hoysala king Vishnuvardhana, besieged the city of Dhorasamudra, pursued him till he arrived at the city of Belápura, which he took, and followed him beyond that as far as the mountain-pass of Váhadi.

Chavunda II., and his sons.

Permádi I. was succeeded by his younger brother Chavunda II. or Chávunda II., a feudatory of the Western Chálukya king Taila III. By his first wife, Demaladevi, Chavunda II. had two sons,—A'chi or A'chugi III., and Pemmádi or Permádi II. We have two inscriptions of his time,—one at Arasibidi, the details of which are very illegible; and one at Pattadakal, dated Saka 1084 for Saka 1085 (A.D. 1163-4), the Subhánu *samvatsara*.[6] At that time he was governing the Kisukád Seventy, the Kelavádi Three-hundred, the Bágadage Seventy, and other districts, while Demaladevi and A'chugi III. were governing as his regents at the city of Pattada-Kisuvolal or Pattadakal. By his second wife Siriyádevi, the sister of the Kalachuri king Bijjala, Chavunda II. had two other sons, Bijjala and Vikrama or Vikramáditya. In an inscription at Aihole, dated Saka 1091 (A.D. 1169-70), the Virodhi *samvatsara*, we find these two brothers governing the Kisukád Seventy, the Bágadage Seventy, and the Kelavádi Three-hundred.[7] This inscription does not mention them as the feudatories of any paramount sovereign; and it is possible that Chavunda II., having intermarried into the

---

1 *Jour. Bo. Br. R. As. Soc.*, Vol. XI., pp. 224 and 239.
2 Elliot *MS. Collection*, Vol. I., p. 440.
3 *Jour. Bo. Br. R. As. Soc.*, Vol. XI., p. 253.
4 An indication that the power of the Sindas extended considerably further than this into the Nizám's Dominions, is given by the name of Sindanur, a large village or town about fifty miles to the east by north from 'Yelburga.'
5 Probably the modern 'Kelludee' of the maps, ten miles to the north by east from Bádámi.
6 *Jour. Bo. Br. R. As. Soc.*, Vol, XI., p. 259; *P. S. and O.-C. Inscriptions*, No. 67.
7 *Jour. Bo. Br. R. As. Soc.*, Vol. XI., p. 274; *P. S. and O.-C. Inscriptions*, No. 83.

B 767

GENEALOGY OF THE SINDAS OF ERAMBARAGE.

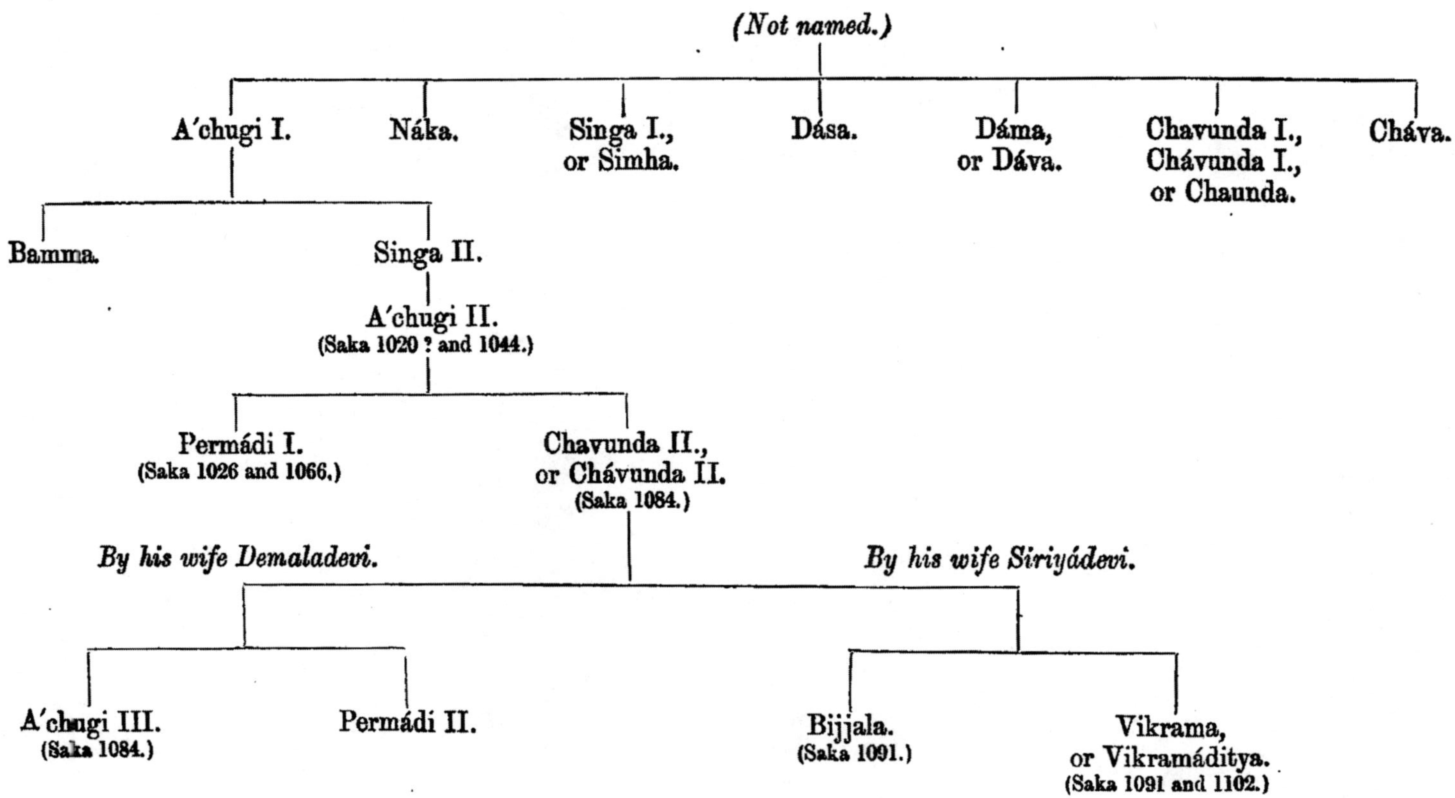

Kalachuri family, enjoyed a short period of independence after the downfall of the Western Chálukyas. But in Saka 1102 (A.D. 1180-1), the Sárvari *samvatsara*, we find Vikrama, at his capital of Erambarage, governing the Kisukád Seventy only, and as the feudatory of the Kalachuri king Sankama.[1] This is the last notice that we have of this branch of the Sinda family.

But there was at least one other branch of it. Thus, at Bhairanmatti in the Kaládgi District there is an inscription, dated Saka 955 (A.D. 1033-4), the Srimukha *samvatsara*, of Nágati or Nágáditya and Sevya of the Sindavamsa, who were the feudatories of the Western Chálukya king Jayasimha III.[2] They deduce their genealogy from a certain king Sinda, who was born in Ahichchhatra, and was the king of the Sindhu country, and was married to a Kadamba princess. And they claim to be of the Nágavamsa or serpent race and to have the title of *Bhogávati-puravar-ádhisvara*, or 'supreme lord of Bhogávati, the best of cities,'[3] and to be entitled to carry the banner of a hooded serpent,[4] and to use the mark or signet of a tiger.[5] And the Tidgundi grant of the Western Chálukya king Vikramáditya VI., dated Saka 1004 (A.D. 1082-3), the Dundubhi *samvatsara*,[6] mentions, as his feudatory, a certain Munja of the Sinda family, who seems to be of the same branch of it with Nágáditya and Sevya, and who, like them, claims to belong to the Nágavamsá and to have the title of 'supreme lord of the city of Bhogávatipura.'

---

1 Elliot *MS. Collection*, Vol. II., pp. 221 and 226.

2 *P. S. and O.-C. Inscriptions*, No. 86; Elliot *MS. Collection*, Vol. I., p. 25.

3 Bhogávati, in mythology, was the capital of the Nága or serpent king Vásuki, in Rasátala, one of the seven divisions of Pátála or the subterranean regions. Prof. Monier Williams gives it also as a name of Ujjayini in the Dvápara age.

4 *Phanipatáka*. 5 *Vyághralánchhana*. 6 *Ind. Ant.*, Vol. I., p. 80.

SECTION XIV.

THE SILA'HA'RAS OF KOLHA'PUR.

There were two branches of the Siláhára family in the northern and the southern divisions of the Konkan. Of the northern branch, notices have been published by Dr. Bühler and other writers.[1] We have already mentioned Kapardi II. of this branch, whose date was Saka 773 (A.D. 851-2) and Saka 799 (A.D. 877-8), in connection with the Ráshtrakuta king Amoghavarsha I., to whom he seems to have been feudatory; and we have also seen that the Kádambas of Goa probably came in conflict with this family between the dates of Saka 946 (A.D. 1024-5) and Saka 982 (A.D. 1060-1). Of the southern branch, the representative in Saka 930 (A.D. 1008-9) was Ráhurája, the feudatory of the Western Chálukya king Satyásraya II.;[2] and this branch of the family possibly preceded the Kádambas of Goa in their possessions in the Konkan.

We are concerned here in detail only with a third branch of the Siláhára family, which was settled above the Ghauts, and the inscriptions of which are found at Kolhápur and places in that neighbourhood, at Miraj, and at Sedbál in the Athani Táluká of the Belgaum District. The members of this branch of the family possessed the territory lying round Kolhápur and in the north-west part of the Belgaum District, from about the end of the tenth to early in the thirteenth century A.D.

Like their relatives of the northern branch in the Konkan, the Siláháras of Kolhápur claim to be of the lineage of the *Vidyádhara* Jimutaváhana, who saved the Nága king Sankhachuda from Garuda by offering his own body to be torn instead of his. And, also like them, they carried the banner of a golden Garuda,[3] and had the title of *Tagara-puravar-ádhisvara*, or 'supreme lord of Tagara, the best of cities.' Tagarapura therefore was the city from which the Siláháras originally started. It is a place, however, that has not yet been satisfactorily identified. It was of sufficient importance to be mentioned in the second century A.D. by Ptolemy, in whose map of India it is entered in a north-easterly direction from Barugaza or Broach, and also, in the third century, by the author of the *Periplus of the Erythræan Sea*, who says that it was ten days journey to the east of Paithana which was twenty days to the south of Barugaza.[4] Paithana,—which appears in Ptolemy's map under the name of Baithana, and, like Tagara, is entered in

---

1 *Ind. Ant.*, Vol. V., p. 276, and Vol. IX., p. 33; *Jour. R. As. Soc.*, O. S., Vol. II., pp. 383 and 386, Vol. IV., p. 109, and Vol. V., p. 176; and *Jour. Bo. Br. R. As. Soc.* Vol. XIII., p. 10.

2 *Jour. Bo. Br. R. As. Soc.*, Vol. I., p. 209.

3 *Suvarnagarudadhvaja.*

4 *Ind. Ant.*, Vol. VIII., p. 144.

an easterly or north-easterly direction from Barugaza,—is usually accepted to be Paithán, the ancient Pratishthána, on the banks of the Godávari, about two hundred and twenty miles to the south-east from Broach. No identification of Tagara, in accordance with the directions and distances mentioned above, has as yet been made. But, on the assumption that the directions and distances are not correct, it has been suggested that Tagara is Devagiri or Daulatábád, about thirty-five miles to the north-west of Paithán; and again that it is Junnár [1] in the Poona District, about one hundred and five miles to the west by south from Paithán.[2] Prof. Lassen and Col. Yule, again, have suggested that it is Kulbarga[3] in the Nizám's Dominions.[4] The fact that it is mentioned, as the residence of the grantee, in the Haidarábád grant of the Western Chalukya king Pulikesi II., dated Saka 534 (A.D. 612-3), and issued from Vátápi or Bádámi,[5] seems to justify us in looking for it more to the south than is usually supposed. And,—though this place appears altogether too far to the south,—in connection with Sir Walter Elliot's remark, that a native trader once told him that, on his way from Dhárwád to Nágpur, he had passed through a good-sized town of this name, with a *bázár* or market and a *nálá* or small river near it, four *coss* beyond Kulbarga,[6] it seems worth noting that there is a village called 'Tagarapuram' in the 'Kollekalam' division of Coimbatore.[7] My own opinion, however, is that Tagara is to be identified with Kolhápur,—or rather with Karavira, which is now only a small village on the north side of Kolhápur, but which, as the native name for the Kolhápur State, *viz.* 'the Karavira Ilákhá,' and also the name of the local *Purána, viz.* 'the Karavira-*Máhátmya*,' are deduced from it, must evidently have been in former times a place of considerably more importance than at present. There is a connection between the two names which is not at first sight apparent. *Tagara* is 'the shrub Tabernæmontana Coronaria,' (and also 'a fragrant powder prepared from it'); [8] it belongs to the same family with the oleander; it is still called *tagar* in Maráthi,[9] and grows freely in this part of the country, though whether it is originally an exotic, or a natural shrub, I cannot say; and the flowers of it are used in the worship of idols. And *karavira* is 'the Nerium Odorum,' the fragrant oleander,[10] which

---

1 Lat. 19° 13' N., Long. 73° 57' E.

2 *Ind. Ant.*, Vol. VIII., p. 144, note.

3 Lat. 17° 21' N., Long. 76° 55' E.

4 Lassen's *Map of Ancient India*; and see Bombay *Third Archæological Report*, p. 55, note.

5 *Ind. Ant.*, Vol. VI., p. 75.

6 *Madras Jour. of Lit. and Science*, Vol. VII., p. 226.

7 *Atlas of Southern India*, Pharaoh & Co., Madras, Plates 6 and 12.—It is in about Lat. 12° 8' N. and Long. 77° 3' E., a little to the west of a line connecting Talakád and Yelendur, both of which are places of note. It is, however, about three hundred and fifty miles from Kulbarga, almost due south.

8 Monier Williams' *Sanskrit Dictionary*, and Childer's *Páli Dictionary*.—C. P. Brown, in his *Telugu Dictionary*, gives *tagara* as 'the tree called Morinda Tinctoria,' but makes it also equivalent to the *nandivardhana-chettu* and *nandyávarta*, which he separately gives as meaning 'the broad-leaved rose bay, Nerium Odorum; Tabernæmontana Grandiflora.' And Monier Williams gives *nandyávarta* as equivalent to *tagara* in the sense of Tabernæmontana Coronaria.

9 Some *Mális*, however, make a distinction, and call the single flower *nandibatla* and only the double flower *tagar*.

10 Monier Williams' *Sanskrit Dictionary*; Childers' *Páli Dictionary*, Sanderson's *Canarese Dictionary*, and Brown's *Telugu Dictionary*.

also grows freely, wild, all over this part of the country, and is similarly used in the worship of idols. Of course, neither the Tabernæmontana Coronaria, nor the Nerium Odorum, is in any way whatever confined to this part of the country. Nor is there now any specially exuberant growth of either of them at Kolhápur. In this latter respect there may, perhaps, have been a difference in ancient times. But, even if so, the botanical connection between the two names, however interesting and suggestive, could hardly, without strong extraneous reasons, be taken to establish the identity of the two places. Some such extraneous reasons, however, of a valid kind, are, I think, forthcoming. *Tagara* is also 'the thorny shrub, Vangueria Spinosa';[1] and *karaháta*, which is the ancient name of the modern Karhád or Karád at the junction of the Krishná and the Koiná in the Sattárá District, is another name of the Vangueria Spinosa.[2] Accordingly, as far as these names go, a connection might be looked for between Tagara and either Karavira or Karhád. Neither of these places agrees with Tagara according to the distance and direction from Paithana or Paithán, as given by the author of the *Periplus of the Erythræan Sea.* But neither do the other two places, Daulatábád and Junnár, which it has been proposed to identify with Tagara, suit in these respects; and it seems to be the general *consensus* of opinion that the distance and direction of Tagara from Paithán are not correctly given. Assuming this,—either Karavira or Karhád would fit in well with the intimation of the author of the *Periplus* that Tagara was an inland mart for "articles of local production, brought into it from the parts along the coast." And either of them would supply what is not otherwise to be supplied from any information that we have, *viz.* a large trade-centre, above but near the Western Ghauts, to collect the ancient trade of this part of the country and also of those parts of the Konkan which lie along immediately under the Ghauts, and which would find a more convenient outlet over the Ghauts than towards the sea-coast. We have as yet discovered no place that could serve as such a trade-centre, for really ancient times, anywhere between Paithán on the Godávari and Palásiká, the modern Halsi in the Belgaum District, about two hundred and eighty miles to the south by west from Paithán. Also, from either Karavira or Karhád, the inland trade route to Broach would, before the systematic construction of roads of modern times, naturally seek the open country lying to the east of the inland spurs of the Ghauts, and thus would naturally pass through Paithán;[3] and this would explain why the author of the *Periplus* refers the position of Tagara to Paithán and not to Broach. And finally,—whether Karhád has, or has not, I cannot say; but Kolhápur still has a considerable import trade, partly for local consumption and partly for export again towards the east, in rice, jowári, wheat, gram, and other grains, salt, oil-seeds, cocoanuts, limes, mangoes, vegetables, and other "articles of local production," with the Ratnágiri District and

---

1 Monier Williams' *Sanskrit Dictionary.* 2 *Idem.*

3 The easiest route from Karavira or Kolhápur would be *viá* Miraj and Pandharpur; and the distance to Paithán would be about two hundred and thirty miles. From Karhád there would be more obstacles to be crossed before reaching the open country; and the distance to Paithán would be only about ten miles less.

the Sáwantwádi State below the Ghauts; and in its own local productions of grain, coriander-seeds, ghee, jaggery, honey, oil, turmeric, tobacco, chillies, &c., Kolhápur has still a considerable export trade with inland places which include, to the north, Ahmadnagar, only some fifty or sixty miles distant from Paithán itself.[1] Of the two places, I prefer Karavira for identification with Tagara for the following reasons. Karhád is nowhere spoken of as a capital of the Siláháras. And, while it was known by the name of Karahátaka in the eighth century A.D.,[2] it also seems to be undoubtedly, as Pandit Bhagwánlál Indraji takes it to be, the Karahákataka of an early Páli cave-inscription at Kudá near Rájápur in the Ratnágiri District;[3] and this carries back the existence of the name to at least as early a period as that of the author of the *Periplus*, and shows moreover that the town was well known under that name at one of the places which the author of the *Periplus* must certainly have visited. Kolhápur, or Karavira, on the other hand, must always have been one of the chief seats of the Silábára power, though it is not expressly mentioned as the capital till Saka 1109 (A.D. 1187-8), in the time of Bhoja II. All tradition points to its being a place of extreme antiquity. And the tradition, in this respect, is borne out by the numerous Buddhist remains that are found at and in the immediate neighbourhood of Kolhápur, and notably by a crystal relic-casket which was found in a large *stupa*, discovered in making some excavations at Kolhápur about two years ago, and the lid of which bears an inscription in pure Maurya or Asoka characters, *i.e.* of about the end of the third century B.C.[4] Graham states[5] that "there are no ruins of any great magnitude, the mementos of any large and flourishing town." And further on he adds,[6] "Kolhapur has long held a high station for the antiquity of her sacred shrines; and all the current legends state that her present capital originally existed as a purely religious settlement, of which the great temple, dedicated to Ambábái or Mahálakshmi, remains to mark the site. The cloisters which formerly surrounded this great temple now lie buried many feet under the surface of the earth, which appears to have undergone at no distant period a very startling convulsion. Many phenomena favour this legend. The tiny temples are frequently brought to light on any excavation being made, and to this day no well for the purpose of irrigation is allowed within the sacred precincts. Two of the subterranean temples over which dwelling-houses have been erected are even now much frequented, one being dedicated to Kárttikasvámi, and the other to Khandobá; and in further support of the oral tradition, that in olden times the dreary jungle was only marked by a multitude of holy temples and holy pools, the spring frequently gushes out when digging for a foundation. Stone slabs, covered with strange figures and ancient inscriptions, are found at a depth of upwards of fifteen feet from the surface; the heights of the same wall of the great temple are

---

1 Graham's *Kolhapoor*, pp. 261 to 268.

2 Sámangad copper-plate grant of the Ráshtrakuta king Dantidurga or Dantivarmá II.; dated Saka 675 (A.D. 753-6).

3 No. 10, p. 16, of the separate pamphlets of the Archæological Survey of Western India.

4 *Id.*, p. 39. 5 *Kolhapoor*, p. 314. 6 *Id.*, pp. 316-7.

unequal at different places; and the ground level is totally altered and destroyed. The convulsion which altered the ancient aspect of affairs must probably have been effected by an earthquake, slight shocks having occurred again during the year 1853. Many geological facts also support this opinion,—in the upheaving of small elevations in the neighbourhood,—in the curious and singular arrangements of the clay about the locality,—and in the existence of the old bed of the river Panchagangá, at an elevation of at least seventy feet above its present level, which was discovered whilst digging for a foundation in the year 1849, and which is clearly evinced by the broad strata of small pebbles, perfectly and smoothly polished, evidently through the action of running water." Yet, in spite of its evident antiquity, whether religious or political, Kolhápur or Karavira is nowhere mentioned under either of those names in any really ancient inscription as yet discovered. I have in fact no epigraphical mention of Karavira at all. And the earliest mention that I have obtained of Kolhápur, under the name of Kollápura, is one of the date of Saka 946 (A.D. 1024-25).[1] Tagara, on the other hand, is mentioned as late as Saka 534 (A.D. 612-3) as the name of a city still in existence.[2] And we have, perhaps, a similar mention of it, of considerably later date, in the Siláhára inscription of Márasimha to be noted below. In it, Jatiga II., whose date would be about the end of the tenth century A.D., is called *Tagaranagara-bhupálaka*, or 'king of the city of Tagara,'—a far more emphatic and specific expression than the usual family-title. This is in a metrical passage; and the usual title of *Tagara-puravar-ádhisvara* would have suited the metre just as well. The expression being at present an isolated one, it is hardly safe to assume conclusively that it was intentionally selected for use in this passage to indicate that Jatiga II. actually reigned at Tagara; from which it would follow that, as late as the end of the tenth century A.D., Tagara was still in use as the name of a city which *must* then have been somewhere in the Kolhápur State or quite close to it. But the expression is certainly fairly open to being construed in that way. However, setting this passage aside for the present, the entire disappearance of Tagara as the name of a still existing city at some time subsequent to the seventh century A.D., and the appearance of Kollápura in the eleventh century A.D. in a neighbourhood in which, equally with others, if not rather than in others, we are entitled to look for Tagara, can, I think, be explained only on the theory of,—first, a complete change of name, such as from Tagara to Karavira, made to suit some mediæval legend, but made in such a way as still to preserve some trace of the original appellation,—and subsequently a change of locality, such as from Karavira to Kollápura. It appears to me that some tradition of an entire change of name having taken place at no very remote period is preserved in the following mythical account given by

---

1 Miraj copper-plate grant of the Western Chálukya king Jayasimha III.—The next mention of it, under the date of Saka 971 (A.D. 1049-50) is in the centre inscription on the south face of the temple of Siddhesvara at Sirur, in the Bágalkot Táluká of the Kaládgi District. The passage is descriptive of the goddess Mahá-lakshmi, "who was established at the *ádi-pitha* of Kollápura, the best of cities."

2 Haidarábád copper-plate grant of the Western Chalukya king Pulikesi II.

Graham from Chapter LVII. of the Karavira-*Máhátmya*:[1]—"This sacred land of Kolhápur has existed from eternity. In seven different ages, it received as many distinct names. As, at one time, it was the residence of Káma, it was termed Kámálaya. At another time it was known as Padmálaya, after the name of its king Padma. In the third age, the god Siva passed his time here in the company of his wife Párvati; and hence it was called Siválaya. In the fourth age, Brahmá gave himself up to devotion in this sacred land of Karavira; and it was then called Brahmálaya. In the fifth age, in consequence of its being the abode of Yakshas, it was designated Yakshálaya. In the sixth age, as the Rákshasas resided here, this place was distinguished by the name of Rákshasálaya. In the seventh or last age, *i. e.* the present, this place was first called Kolhápur and then Karavira." In this passage the name of Kolhápur is made to precede that of Karavira. But, according to other accounts,[2] "this tract of country was originally called Karavira, from the goddess Mahálakshmi using her mace[3] in lifting this, her favoured retreat, from the waters of the great deluge. And it afterwards received the name of Kolhápur from the demon Kola, who was defeated and killed on a hill in the vicinity of the present capital." I am not prepared at present to suggest the correct etymology of the name Kollápura. But it seems plain to me that Karavira is the older and more important name of the two. And, after the change of name from Tagara to Karavira, the transfer of the political capital, from Karavira to the originally religious settlement of Kolhápur, may have been necessitated by some convulsion of nature such as that the indications of which are given very plainly by Graham; and the evidently serious character of that convulsion would explain why no ruins of a large ancient town have been discovered at Kolhápur or at Karavira.

The Siláháras of Kolhápur were Jains by religion. Their family-goddess was Mahálakshmi of Kollápura or Kolhápur; and, though this town is not expressly mentioned as their capital till Saka 1109 (A.D. 1187-8), it must always have been one of the chief seats of their power, and it furnishes the most convenient appellation of this branch of the family, for distinguishing it from the other branches. Their genealogy is as given in the accompanying table.

Márasimha.

All that is at present known about the earlier members of the family is derived from a copper-plate grant of Márasimha, also called Gonkana-Ankakára and Guheyana-Singa, which was found somewhere in the neighbourhood of Miraj and is dated Saka 980 (A.D. 1058-9), the Vilambi *samvatsara*.[4] In it, Jatiga I. is called 'the lion of the hill-fort of Pannála,' which is about ten miles to

---

1 *Kolhapoor*, p. 341.—The way in which the local *Máhátmyas*, intrinsically of no historical value at all, may nevertheless be used to authenticate history, especially in the identification of ancient names of places, has been indicated by me in my identification of Vátápi and Bádámi (*Ind. Ant.*, Vol. VIII., pp. 238-9).

2 *Kolhapoor*, p. 1.

3 Graham gives in brackets the word *karu*; but I do not find that this word has anywhere the meaning of 'a mace.' The passage seems to be a play upon *karavira* in the sense of 'a sword or scimetar.'

4 *Jour. R. As. Soc.*, O. S., Vol. II., p. 384, and Vol. IV., p. 281; and No. 10, p. 101, of the separate pamphlets of the Archæological Survey of Western India.

the north-west of Kolhápur; Jatiga II. is called 'the king of the city of Tagara,' as has been mentioned above; and Gonka is described as possessing the countries of Karaháta, Kundi, Mirinja, and the Konkana. Karaháta is the modern Karád or Karhád[1] in the Sattárá District, at the junction of the Krishná and the Koiná; and Mirinja is the modern Miraj[2] about thirty miles in a north-easterly direction from Kolhápur. Kundi is the Three-thousand district which in Saka 902 (A.D. 980-1) constituted the government of Kártavirya I., of the Ratta *Mahámandalesvaras* of Saundatti, and which, so far as the Ratta inscriptions go, was still entirely in the possession of that family in Saka 970 (A. D. 1048-9), in the time of Anka, and again in Saka 1004 (A.D. 1082-3), in the time of Kannakaira II.; but, unless this statement of Gonka holding the country of Kundi is an invention or an exaggeration, the Rattas must, shortly before or after Saka 970, have suffered some temporary loss of territory to which no allusion is made in their own inscriptions. And the possession by Gonka of part of the Konkana,—probably in the time of Nágárjuna of the north Konkana branch of the Siláháras, who was intermediate between Chhittarája (Saka 946; A.D. 1024-5), and Mummuni or Mumváni (Saka 982; A.D. 1060-1), and as to the events of whose reign the inscriptions of his family are silent,—is corroborated by a passage concerning Anantapála or Anantadeva, the son of Nágárjuna, which has already been quoted to show that the king of Kápardikadvipa who was killed by Jayakesi I., of the Kádambas of Goa, must have been Nágárjuna, and in which the expression "a time of misfortune from relatives that had become hostile" plainly shows that Jayakesi I., who then overran and devastated the whole of that part of the Konkana, had taken advantage of dissensions and contests between the Siláháras of the Konkana and their relatives of Kolhápur. In the same inscription of Márasimha, Guvala I. or Guhala is called 'the lord of the hill-fort of Kiligila or Khiligila;' this place, which was also Márasimha's capital, has not yet been identified. Like his successors, Márasimha styles himself only a *Mahámandalesvara*, but gives no indication of any paramount sovereign of whom he was the feudatory. It is not likely, however, that the Siláháras were independent throughout the whole of the period for which we have records of them. The Silháára princess Chandaladevi or Chandralekhá, who was one of the wives of the Western Chálukya king Vikramáditya VI., was probably a daughter of Márasimha.

Bhoja I.

The next name in respect of which we have any historical information is that of Bhoja I. He seems to be undoubtedly the Bhoja who invaded the territories of A'chugi I., of the family of the Sinda *Mahámandalesvaras* of Erambarage, and who was successfully repulsed by A'chugi; this must have been in about Saka 1020 (A.D. 1098-9).

Ballála.

There is an inscription of Ballála at Honnur near Kágal, which intimates that he ruled in conjunction with his younger brother Gandaráditya.[3] But it is not dated; and it gives no historical information.

---

1 Lat. 17° 18′ N., Long. 74° 14′ E. 2 Lat. 16° 50′ N., Long. 74° 43′ E.
3 Graham's *Kolhapoor*, p. 466.

GENEALOGY OF THE SILA'HA'RAS OF KOLHA'PUR.

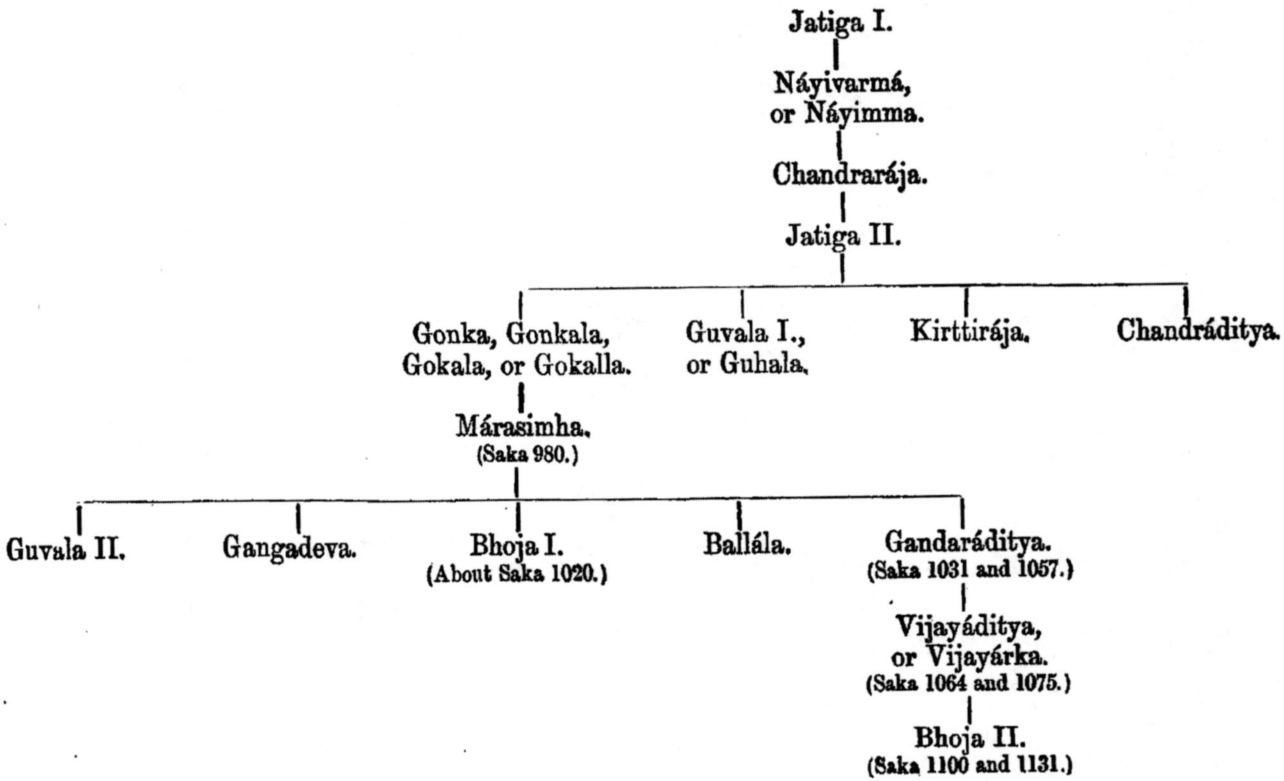

Gandaráditya.

The succession was continued by Gandaráditya, also called Ayyana-Singa I., the youngest son of Márasimha. His inscriptions range from Saka 1032 for 1031 (A.D. 1109-10), the Virodhi *samvatsara*, to Saka 1058 for 1057 (A.D. 1135-6), the Rákshasa *samvatsara*, and are found at Kolhápur itself and at Tálalem in the neighbourhood.[1] In Saka 1031, he was governing the Mirinja country, together with Saptakholla and a part of the Konkana, and his capital was Tiraváda in the Edenád district.[2] In Saka 1057, his capital was Valaváda, which, as suggested by Sir Walter Elliot, is probably the modern Wálwá,[3] about sixteen miles to the south of Kolhápur.

Vijayáditya.

Gandaráditya was succeeded by his son Vijayáditya or Vijayárka, also called Ayyana-Singa II., whose inscriptions range from Saka 1065 for 1064 (A.D. 1142-3), the Dundubhi *samvatsara*, to Saka 1078 for 1075 (A.D. 1153-4), the Srimukha *samvatsara*, and are found at Kolhápur, Miraj, Bámni near Kágal, and Sedbál in the Belgaum District.[4] His capital continued to be at Valaváda. In the copper-plate grant of his son and successor Bhoja II., Vijayáditya is said to have reinstated the rulers of the province of Sthánaka or Thána and the kings of Gová or Goa. The first statement must refer to some assistance rendered by him to his relatives of the Konkana branch, after the reign of Anantapála or Anantadeva and before the reign of Aparáditya; and it was probably through this assistance that Aparáditya came to reign at all. The date that is usually allotted to Aparáditya is Saka 1109 (A.D. 1187-8):[5] but, that this must have been towards the *end* of his reign, and that he was reigning between Saka 1058 and 1068 (A.D. 1135-1145), has been shown by Dr. Bühler;[6] and this proves almost conclusively that it was Aparáditya whom Vijayáditya reinstated at Sthánaka. The statement regarding the kings of Gová,—if it refers to any events affecting Goa itself, and unless it simply means that the Konkana Siláháras continued to bear the title of kings of Gová, though the place itself was lost to them,—must allude to some occurrences between the time of Jayakesi II. and Permádi or Sivachitta, of the Kádambas of Goa, to which no reference is made in the Kádamba inscriptions or in any others that have as yet come to notice.

Bhoja II.

Vijayáditya was succeeded by his son Bhoja II., also called Vijayádityadevana-Singa, whose inscriptions range from Saka 1101 for 1100 (A. D. 1178-9), the Vilambi *samvatsara*, to Saka 1115 (A. D. 1193-4), the Pramádi or Pramádicha *samvatsara*. His

---

1 *Jour. Bo. Br. R. As. Soc.*, Vol. XIII., p. 1.; and unpublished inscriptions, of which imperfect versions are given in Graham's *Kolhapoor*, pp. 326 to 480.

2 This, of course, must be a totally different district to the Edenád Seventy which is mentioned in inscriptions at Balagámve (*P. S. and O.-C. Inscriptions*, No. 158) Sorab (*Mysore Inscriptions*, p. 239), Merkara (*Ind. Ant.*, Vol. I., p. 365), and Bengalur (*Mysore Inscriptions*, p. 294), and which is placed by Mr. Rice near Ságar in Maisur.

3 Lat. 16° 29′ N., Long. 74° 14′ E.—Possibly, however, it may be the 'Wuleewur of the maps, about five miles to the east by north of Kolhápur,—or the 'Wulewra' and 'Wulewday' of the maps, about six miles to the south-west of Wálwá.

4 Unpublished inscriptions; and Graham's *Kolhapoor*.

5 *Ind. Ant.*, Vol. X., pp. 39 &c.

6 *Jour. Bo. Br. R. As. Soc.*, Vol. XII., Extra Number, p. 52.

stone-tablets are found at Kolhápur;[1] and a copper-plate grant of his reign has been produced from somewhere in the Sattárá District.[2] In Saka 1100, Valaváda was his capital; but in Saka 1109, his capital was Kollápura, the modern Kolhápur itself, and in Saka 1112, it was Pannáladurga, or, as the Sanskrit version of the name is, Padmanáladurga, the hill-fort about ten miles to the north-west of Kolhápur. That he was still reigning in Saka 1127 (A.D. 1205-6), the Krodhana *samvatsara,* is shewn by a note at the end of the *Sabdárnavachandriká* of Somadeva, according to which the work was composed in that year, in the reign of Bhoja II., at a Jain temple founded by Gandaráditya at A'juriká, the modern A'jrá, in the country of Kollápura.[3]

With the exception of what has been noted above in connection with Vijayáditya, the inscriptions of Gandaráditya and his successors give no historical details. But, as regards the termination of their power, we have not got the name of any member of the family after Bhoja II. And,—as in Saka 1135 (A.D. 1213-4), the Srimukha *samvatsara,* the Devagiri-Yádava king Singhana II. was in possession of the country round Miraj, as is proved by his Khedrápur inscription,[4] which records the grant by him of the village of Kudaladámaváda, the modern Kurandvád, in the Mirinji country; and as we find inscriptions of Singhana II., shortly after that date, at Kolhápur itself,[5]—it would seem that Bhoja II. was the last of his family, and that he was overthrown and dispossessed by Singhana II., in or soon after Saka 1131 (A.D. 1219-20), the Sukla *samvatsara,* which was the commencement of Singhana's reign. This is borne out by one of Singhana's inscriptions, dated Saka 1160,[6] which speaks of him as having been "a very Garuda in putting to flight the serpent which was the mighty king Bhoja, whose habitation was Pannála."[7]

1 Graham's *Kolhapoor,* pp. 382 to 414.
2 *Transactions of the Literary Society of Bombay,* reprint of 1877, Vol. III., p. 411.
3 Dr. Kielhorn; *Ind. Ant.,* Vol. X., p. 75.
4 *Jour. Bo. Br. R. As. Soc.,* Vol. XII., p. 7.
5 Graham's *Kolhapoor,* pp. 425 to 436.
6 *P. S. and O.-C. Inscriptions,* No. 112, l. 10-11.
7 *Pamnála-nilaya-prabala-Bhojabhupála-vyála-vidrávana-Vihamgarája.*